Mastering Environmental Law

Carolina Academic Press Mastering Series

Russell Weaver, Series Editor

For other titles, please go to caplaw.com.

Mastering Administrative Law, Second Edition
Linda D. Jellum

Mastering Adoption Law and Policy
Cynthia Hawkins DeBose

Mastering Alternative Dispute Resolution
Kelly M. Feeley, James A. Sheehan

Mastering American Indian Law
Angelique Wambdi EagleWoman, Stacy L. Leeds

Mastering Appellate Advocacy and Process, Revised Printing
Donna C. Looper, George W. Kuney

Mastering Art Law
Herbert Lazerow

Mastering Bankruptcy
George W. Kuney

Mastering Civil Procedure, Third Edition
David Charles Hricik

Mastering Constitutional Law, Second Edition
John C. Knechtle, Christopher J. Roederer

Mastering Contract Law
Irma S. Russell, Barbara K. Bucholtz

Mastering Corporate Tax, Second Edition
Gail Levin Richmond, Reginald Mombrun, Felicia Branch

Mastering Corporations and Other Business Entities, Second Edition
Lee Harris

Mastering Criminal Law, Second Edition
Ellen S. Podgor, Peter J. Henning, Neil P. Cohen

Mastering Criminal Procedure, Volume 1:
The Investigative Stage, Second Edition
Peter J. Henning, Andrew Taslitz, Margaret L. Paris, Cynthia E. Jones, Ellen S. Podgor

Mastering Criminal Procedure, Volume 2:
The Adjudicatory Stage, Second Edition
Peter J. Henning, Andrew Taslitz, Margaret L. Paris, Cynthia E. Jones, Ellen S. Podgor

Mastering Elder Law, Second Edition
Ralph C. Brashier

Mastering Employment Discrimination Law, Second Edition
Paul M. Secunda, Jeffrey M. Hirsch, Joseph A. Seiner

Mastering Environmental Law
Joel A. Mintz, Tracy Hester

Mastering First Amendment Law
John C. Knechtle

Mastering Income Tax
Christopher M. Pietruszkiewicz, Gail Levin Richmond

Mastering Intellectual Property
George W. Kuney, Donna C. Looper

Mastering Labor Law
Paul M. Secunda, Anne Marie Lofaso, Joseph E. Slater, Jeffrey M. Hirsch

Mastering Legal Analysis and Drafting
George W. Kuney, Donna C. Looper

Mastering Negotiable Instruments (UCC Articles 3 and 4) and Other Payment Systems, Second Edition
Michael D. Floyd

Mastering Negotiation
Michael R. Fowler

Mastering Partnership Taxation
Stuart Lazar

Mastering Professional Responsibility, Second Edition
Grace M. Giesel

Mastering Property Law, Revised Printing
Darryl C. Wilson, Cynthia Hawkins DeBose

Mastering Sales
Colin P. Marks, Jeremy Kidd

Mastering Secured Transactions: UCC Article 9, Second Edition
Richard H. Nowka

Mastering Statutory Interpretation, Second Edition
Linda D. Jellum

Mastering Tort Law, Second Edition
Russell L. Weaver, Edward C. Martin, Andrew R. Klein, Paul J. Zwier, II, John H. Bauman

Mastering Trademark and Unfair Competition Law
Lars S. Smith, Llewellyn Joseph Gibbons

Mastering Trusts and Estates
Gail Levin Richmond, Don Castleman

For other titles, please go to caplaw.com.

Mastering Environmental Law

Joel A. Mintz
Professor of Law Emeritus
C. William Trout Senior Fellow
Nova Southeastern University
Shepard Broad College of Law

Tracy D. Hester
Instructional Professor of Law
University of Houston Law Center

Carolina Academic Press
Durham, North Carolina

Library of Congress Cataloging-in-Publication Data

Names: Mintz, Joel A., 1949- author. | Hester, Tracy, author.
Title: Mastering environmental law / by Joel A. Mintz and Tracy Hester.
Description: Durham, North Carolina : Carolina Academic Press, LLC, 2019. | Series: Mastering series
Identifiers: LCCN 2019003156 | ISBN 9781531000905 (alk. paper)
Subjects: LCSH: Environmental law--United States.
Classification: LCC KF3775 .M584 2019 | DDC 344.7304/6--dc23
LC record available at https://lccn.loc.gov/2019003156

eISBN: 978-1-5310-0091-2

Carolina Academic Press, LLC
700 Kent Street
Durham, North Carolina 27701
Telephone (919) 489-7486
Fax (919) 493-5668
www.cap-press.com

Printed in the United States of America

To my wonderful mother and the memory of my father,
my first teachers and truly marvelous role models.
—J.A.M.

To Linda, who effortlessly combines being my wife,
my best friend, my colleague, and my inspiration.
—T.D.H.

Contents

Table of Cases

Series Editor's Foreword

The Carolina Academic Press Mastering Series is designed to provide you with a tool that will enable you to easily and efficiently "master" the substance and content of law school courses. Throughout the series, the focus is on quality writing that makes legal concepts understandable. As a result, the series is designed to be easy to read and is not unduly cluttered with footnotes or cites to secondary sources.

In order to facilitate student mastery of topics, the Mastering Series includes a number of pedagogical features designed to improve learning and retention. At the beginning of each chapter, you will find a "Roadmap" that tells you about the chapter and provides you with a sense of the material that you will cover. A "Checkpoint" at the end of each chapter encourages you to stop and review the key concepts, reiterating what you have learned. Throughout the book, key terms are explained and emphasized. Finally, a "Master Checklist" at the end of each book reinforces what you have learned and helps you identify any areas that need review or further study.

We hope that you will enjoy studying with, and learning from, the Mastering Series.

Russell L. Weaver
Professor of Law & Distinguished University Scholar
University of Louisville, Louis D. Brandeis School of Law

Mastering Environmental Law

Chapter 1

Introduction

Contemporary domestic Environmental Law has evoked a crowd of adjectives: controversial, important, ambitious, idealistic, consequential, enforceable, interdisciplinary, voluminous, and (at least somewhat) politicized. To an extent, Environmental Law certainly is all of these things. It is also a branch of the law that has significant implications for Administrative Law, human health, international relations, and the American economy. Moreover, it is a legal specialty that is, at the same time, challenging and enjoyable to practice.

Environmental attorneys practice in a variety of settings. Most of them work in the offices of government agencies, prosecutors, legislators, private law firms, corporations, and public interest environmental organizations. Their tasks also vary considerably. Environmental lawyers may specialize in a particular branch of environmental law (e.g., hazardous waste requirements or air pollution control standards) or pursue general environmental law practices that embrace all (or nearly all) subcomponents of the field. Environmental lawyers draft legislation, write and revise administrative agency regulations, pursue enforcement actions against environmental polluters, defend clients in environmental enforcement cases, counsel private clients to avoid environmental liabilities, lobby legislative bodies and agencies on behalf of their clients, handle the environmental aspects of real estate and corporate transactions, and engage in myriad other legal work that affects public health and the natural environment.

This book aims to provide a broad overview of the most important legal principles in Environmental Law at the federal level. As you'll observe, this body of law has a very important statutory and regulatory component. The U.S. Environmental Protection Agency (EPA) plays a fundamental role in implementing the federal pollution control requirements mandated by Congress. When mandated (or simply authorized) to do so, EPA writes specific regulations that carry out Congress' directives. In coordination with the U.S. Department of Justice (DOJ), state and local governments, and private citizens, EPA also brings enforcement actions where it becomes aware of instances of noncompliance with environmental laws by private firms or local governmental bodies.

As you will see, most environmental legislation relies on an arrangement referred to as "cooperative federalism." Environmental statutes thus allocate significant responsibilities to state and local governments and to private citizens in implementing the goals of the various statutes.

This book provides an introductory overview of important substantive and broadly applicable aspects of Environmental Law, as well as certain federal laws that are more narrowly focused. Topics that apply more widely are treated in the chapters on Environmental Enforcement, Environmental Litigation, and the National Environmental Policy Act. Other chapters focus on such relatively specialized subjects as air pollution control, climate change, control of water pollution, clean-ups of facilities that have been contaminated with hazardous substances, the handling and proper disposal of dangerous waste materials, the manufacture of toxic chemical products, regulation of pesticides, and protection of endangered species.

Whether you are a law student, an attorney with limited experience with the intricacies of Environmental Law, or a general reader, we hope this book will provide you with a concise introduction to our field. If you find the subject matter even a fraction as fascinating as it has long been to us co-authors, our work will not have been in vain.

Chapter 2

The Clean Air Act

Roadmap

- Understand the role of common law approaches to air pollution control.
- Learn what criteria pollutants are.
- Comprehend how National Ambient Air Quality Standards are established.
- Understand how State Implementation Plans are devised as a means of regulating criteria pollutants.
- Learn the Clean Air Act's approach to limiting emissions of hazardous air pollutants.
- Grasp the requirements that apply to new and modified sources of air pollution in clean air (attainment areas) and dirty air (nonattainment areas).
- Comprehend Clean Air Act requirements that pertain to air pollution from motor vehicles.

I. Introduction and Overview

Air pollution presents serious problems for public health, property, and the natural environment. It has been linked to increases in premature deaths and in rates of illness—particularly among babies and infants, the elderly, and people with preexisting respiratory or cardiac conditions. It also may inflict extensive and costly damage on buildings, materials, and food crops and other plants, and it may dim visibility.

In this chapter, we will examine the United States' legal response to the air pollution problem. After considering the private common law of air pollution, we will focus on key facets of the Clean Air Act, an important, comprehensive federal statute that was passed (in its modern form) in 1970, and amended by Congress in 1977 and 1990.

We will look first at the Act's scheme for regulating "criteria pollutants," the most common types of air pollution, through the establishment of national standards of outdoor air purity (the so-called "National Ambient Air

Quality Standards" or "NAAQS"), and State Implementation Plans ("SIPs"), i.e., state-by-state requirements intended to attain (or maintain) NAAQS by establishing enforceable air pollution control requirements. We will then turn to the controls on hazardous air pollutants mandated by the Act. From there, we will focus on the Clean Air Act's treatment of new sources of air pollution, both in dirty air areas in which NAAQS have not been attained and in clean air regions where those ambient air quality standards are being attained. Finally, we will consider the way in which this legislation imposes controls on air pollution emitted by motor vehicles.

II. Common Law Approaches to Air Pollution Control

While most modern law of air pollution control is based upon federal legislation, the common law doctrines of nuisance and trespass have retained vitality as sources of law regarding air pollution problems. Along with local smoke ordinances, these doctrines were the foundations of the Clean Air Act. The earliest smoke abatement legislation was enacted in London in the thirteenth century, and private common law actions regarding air pollution have their roots in early English common law.

One issue that has arisen in modern air pollution nuisance cases involves the remedy to be awarded to a prevailing plaintiff. In *Boomer v. Atlantic Cement Co.*, 257 N.E.2d 870 (1970), the New York Court of Appeals declined to enjoin the operation of a cement plant that was damaging adjoining properties by emitting smoke and vibrations onto them. Although the plant's activities were creating a private nuisance, the court took note of the fact that the total damage to the plaintiff's properties was relatively small in comparison with the value of the defendant's operation and the consequences of issuing an injunction. As a result, over a vigorous dissent, the court required the defendant to instead pay permanent damages to the plaintiffs to compensate them for their present and future property losses.

The U.S. Supreme Court took a different approach in a public nuisance case, *Georgia v. Tennessee Copper Co.*, 237 U.S. 474 (1915). There, air pollutants from a copper smelter were harming some nearby small farms. The Court granted an injunction but allowed the defendant smelting company time to devise a technological solution to its emission problem. In the meanwhile, the Court established a claims process to compensate the plaintiff farmers. This judicial approach presaged the "technology forcing" policy of the Clean Air Act discussed below.

Another remedial approach in air pollution nuisance matters, adopted by the Supreme Court of Arizona, is the "compensated injunction." In most states, no recovery is permitted in a nuisance case where the plaintiff has "come to the nuisance," i.e., located its development in a community after a nuisance was already in place. In *Spur Industries, Inc. v. Del Webb Development Co.*, 494 P.2d 700 (Ariz. 1972), however, the court created an exception to that doctrine. It enjoined the operation of a smelly cattle feedlot that had been present in a rural part of Arizona before a retirement community was built close to it. However, it also required the plaintiff retirement community developer to reimburse the feedlot owner for the expense of moving or closing.

Although state common law claims generally remain available to redress air pollution problems, federal common law claims have been displaced where the Clean Air Act empowers EPA to regulate the pollutant in question. This is the case with respect to both claims for damages and requests for injunctive relief. *See Native Village of Kivalina v. Exxon-Mobil Corp.*, 639 F.3d 849 (9th Cir. 2012); and *American Electric Power Co., Inc. v. Connecticut*, 564 U.S. 410 (2011).

III. The Clean Air Act

A. National Ambient Air Quality Standards and State Implementation Plans

1. Setting National Ambient Air Quality Standards

The Clean Air Act creates several distinct sets of requirements for the control of air pollution from stationary sources (like factory smokestacks) and mobile sources (such as cars and trucks). A central part of the Act calls for the regulation of "criteria pollutants," i.e., air pollutants from different sources that may reasonably be anticipated to endanger public health or welfare. Clean Air Act § 108, 42 U.S.C. § 7408. The U.S. Environmental Protection Agency ("EPA" or "the Agency") was initially required to identify such pollutants, and to prepare "air quality criteria" documents for each of them that indicate their effects on public health and welfare, and the techniques available to prevent or control their emissions. *Id.* EPA has done this with respect to six commonly emitted air pollutants: sulfur dioxide, nitrogen oxide, carbon monoxide, ozone, suspended particulate matter, and lead.

After identifying criteria pollutants, and reporting on their impacts and possible controls, EPA must establish National Ambient Air Quality Standards

(NAAQS) for each criteria pollutant. These standards are to reflect the levels of outdoor air purity that are neither necessary to protect public health and public welfare. Health-based standards are referred to as "primary standards." Welfare-protective standards are known as "secondary standards." Clean Air Act § 109, 42 U.S.C. § 7904.

In contrast to other parts of the Clean Air Act, and other environmental statutes, it has been firmly established that considerations of economic cost may play no part in the promulgation of NAAQS. The protection of public health "with an adequate margin of safety" is the only pertinent factor to be used in setting those standards. *Lead Industries Association, Inc. v. EPA*, 647 F.2d 1130 (D.C. Cir. 1980); *Whitman v. American Trucking Association, Inc.*, 531 U.S. 457 (2001).

Although they are often controversial, and frequently challenged in lawsuits, EPA's NAAQS have generally fared well under judicial review. A paradigmatic illustration of this is *Lead Industries Association, Inc. v. EPA*, 647 F.2d 1130 (D.C. Cir. 1980), in which the D.C. Circuit upheld the health-and welfare-based standards the Agency had established for lead. Rejecting the industry challengers' contentions, the court declared that "requiring EPA to wait until it can conclusively demonstrate that a particular effect is adverse to health before it acts is inconsistent with both the Act's precautionary and preventative orientation and the nature of the [EPA] Administrator's statutory responsibilities." *Id.* The court went on to review the agency's lead NAAQS and supporting data in considerable detail, concluding that the standards were based on sound decisions regarding the health effects of lead, and did not exceed the adequate margin of safety required by the statute. The court also accepted EPA's conclusion that a secondary standard for lead more stringent than the primary standard was necessary. *Id.*

2. *What Must a State Implementation Plan Contain?*

Once EPA has established NAAQS for criteria pollutants, individual states are required to identify air quality control regions within their borders that do and do not meet the standards. Clean Air Act, § 110, 42 U.S.C. § 7410. Regions whose air quality meets the NAAQS for a pollutant are considered "attainment areas" for the pollutant in question. Areas where the standards are not being met are referred to as "nonattainment areas."

Each state must then adopt a State Implementation Plan ("SIP") containing enforceable emissions limitations that will result in the attainment and maintenance of NAAQS in all air quality control regions within the state. *Id.* SIPs must meet a detailed list of conditions set forth in the statute; and they must be the subject of a public hearing prior to their adoption. Clean Air Act § 110(a)(2), 42 U.S.C. § 7410(a)(2).

Once a state has adopted a SIP, it must submit its plan to EPA for approval (in whole or part), conditional approval, or disapproval. Where the Agency determines that a state's plan is not consistent with the Act's requirements—or a state entirely fails to submit a plan—EPA is authorized to adopt a binding Federal Implementation Plan ("FIP") for the state.

SIPs and FIPs generally contain specific and detailed substantive requirements governing the types and amounts of air pollutants that pollution sources are permitted to emit under both federal and state law. They are the source of many of the provisions incorporated in permits issued to individual emitting facilities, and they may be enforced by EPA (through the U.S. Department of Justice), state officials, and private citizens. *See* Clean Air Act § 110(a)(1), 42 U.S.C. § 7410(a)(1); Clean Air Act § 110(c)(1), 42 U.S.C. § 7410(c)(1); and Clean Air Act § 304, U.S.C. § 7604.

In nonattainment areas, SIPs must require already-existing stationary sources of air pollution to make use of "reasonably available control technology" ("RACT"), which is generally defined through the application of "Control Techniques Guidelines" ("CTGs") prepared by EPA. The latter describe RACT for particular kinds of sources, and the levels of controls that the technology in question may be expected to achieve. Moreover, nonattainment area SIPs must also contain any additional control measures for existing sources (such as fees, marketable permits, and auctions of emission rights) that are necessary to attain NAAQS. Clean Air Act §§ 172(c)(1), (2), and (3), 42 U.S.C. §§ 7502(c)(1), (2), and (3).

The Clean Air Act reflects an underlying theory of "technology-forcing," i.e., the legislation is designed to force regulated sources to develop and make use of pollution control devices that appear to be economically or technologically infeasible at the time applicable standards are established. As a result, the U.S. Supreme Court has held that claims of economic and technology infeasibility must be "wholly foreign" to EPA's review of a state-proposed SIP, and such claims may not be raised on judicial review. *Union Electric Co. v. EPA*, 427 U.S. 246 (1976).

The statute also contains a provision, commonly known as the "Good Neighbor Provision," that is intended to tackle the complex problem of efficiently and equitably controlling air pollution that is emitted in one state and causes harm in one or more other states. The Act mandates that upwind states design their SIPs to prohibit in-state sources "from emitting any air pollutant in amounts which will . . . contribute significantly" to downwind states' "nonattainment . . . or interfere with maintenance" of any NAAQS. *See* Clean Air Act § 110(a)(2)(D)(i), 42 U.S.C. § 7410(a)(2)(D)(i). In response to this provision, EPA devised a rule ("the Transport Rule") to define what constitutes a "significant contribution" to downwind state nonattainment. First, an upwind state must produce one percent or more of an NAAQS in at least one downward state. And second, to constitute a significant contribution, the upwind state's cross-border air pollution must be capable of "cost-effective" elimination (as determined by EPA). This rule was upheld by the U.S. Supreme Court in *Environmental Protection Agency v. EME Homer Generation*, 134 S. Ct. 1584 (2014). The Court pronounced the rule both efficient and equitable since it achieves the required emission reductions at a lower overall cost while also subjecting states that have done relatively less in the past to control their pollution to stricter regulation. *Id.*

B. Regulation of Hazardous Air Pollutants

The initial approach to the control of hazardous air pollutants—also sometimes called "air toxins" or "HAPs"—required EPA to establish health-based standards for individual pollutants from specific sources. These regulations were referred to as National Emission Standards for Hazardous Air Pollutants ("NESHAPS"), and some of those standards remain in force today. *See* 40 C.F.R. pt. 61. Perhaps the most significant of the NESHAPS is the standard for asbestos demolition and renovation, which requires that asbestos be handled using specific workplace techniques. *See* 40 C.F.R. § 61.1145(c)(2). This regulation has been the basis for a significant number of federal criminal enforcement cases.

When the Clean Air Act was amended in 1990, however, Congress established a new, more comprehensive approach to the regulation of HAPs. The amended Act included a list of 189 specific toxic substances that were presumed to require strict control. *See* Clean Air Act § 112(b)(1), 42 U.S.C. § 7412(b)(1). EPA was required to publish a list of all categories and subcategories of "major sources" of the toxic substances listed in the statute, and to establish technology-based emissions standards for each such category or sub-category for both new and hazardous pollutant sources. Clean Air Act §§ 112(c)(1) and (2), 42 U.S.C. §§ 7412(c)(1) and (2). The Agency must also periodically review Congress' list of air toxins and add to that list when an unlisted pollutant is found to threaten adverse effects on human health or the environment. Clean Air Act § 112(b)(2), 42 U.S.C. § 7412(b)(2). In addition, "any person" is permitted to petition EPA for the addition or deletion of any substance from the statutory air toxins list; and the Agency may add or delete a substance from the list upon a persuasive showing that the substance may or may not reasonably be anticipated to cause "any adverse effects to the human health or adverse environmental effects." Clean Air Act § 112(b)(3), 42 U.S.C. § 7412(b)(3).

The amended Clean Air Act set forth a timetable for EPA to adhere to in establishing standards for HAPs. *See* Clean Air Act § 112(e), 42 U.S.C. § 7412(e). For major sources, those standards were to be based upon the maximum available control technology ("MACT"). With regard to new major sources, MACT standards must reflect the level of emission control achieved in practice by the best controlled similar sources. Clean Air Act § 112(d)(3), 42 U.S.C. § 7412(d)(3). MACT standards for existing sources of air toxins may be less stringent than new source MACT requirements, but they must nonetheless be within specific statutorily prescribed limitations. *Id.* And EPA is authorized to promulgate less demanding standards, based upon "generally available control technologies or management practices" ("GACT") for smaller sources—known as "area sources"—that are too small to be classified as major sources of HAPs. Clean Air Act § 112(d)(5), 42 U.S.C. § 7412(d)(5).

The statute also requires EPA to study and report to Congress on any public health risks that will remain after MACT standards have been implemented and on "the technologically and commercially available methods and costs of reducing such risks." Clean Air Act § 112(f), 42 U.S.C. § 7412(f). Where Congress fails to act on any recommendation contained in this EPA report, the Agency may then set additional standards regarding air toxin emissions that will further protect public health "with an ample margin of safety." Clean Air Act § 112(f)(2), 42 U.S.C. § 7412(f)(2).

EPA's definitions of "major sources" within particular industrial categories and sub-categories have been the subject of litigation. For example, in *National Mining Association v. United States Environmental Protection Agency*, 59 F.3d 1351 (D.C. Cir. 1995) industry petitioners challenged an EPA decision to determine whether a site is a major source by taking account of all emissions from the site that are on a contiguous plant site under common control. The court rejected the petitioners' contentions, concluding that "EPA's definition of major source . . . is faithful to the language of [Clean Air Act] § 112(a)(1). . . ." *Id.* On the other hand, a divided U.S. Supreme Court remanded EPA's regulations regarding hazardous air pollutants from power plants on the basis that the Agency had failed to find that such regulations were "appropriate and necessary" when it did not consider cost in its initial decision to develop those regulations. *See Michigan v. Environmental Protection Agency*, 135 S. Ct. 2699 (2015).

C. Requirements Applying to New Sources of Air Pollution

1. Limitations on New Sources in "Nonattainment Areas"

New and modified stationary sources of air pollution in designated nonattainment areas must meet two sets of Clean Air Act requirements: New Source Performance Standards ("NSPS") and New Source Review (NSR). To establish an NSPS, EPA is required to publish (and from time to time revise) a list of categories of stationary sources that cause or contribute significantly to air pollution "which may reasonably be anticipated to endanger public health or welfare." Clean Air Act § 111(b)(1)(A), 42 U.S.C. § 7411(b)(1)(A). EPA must then propose and promulgate "standards of performance" for the listed categories. These standards must reflect "the degree of emission limitation achievable through the application of the best system of emission reduction which (taking into account the cost of achieving such reduction and any non-air quality health or environmental impact and energy requirements) the [EPA] Administrator determines has been adequately demonstrated." Clean Air Act § 111(a)(1), 42 U.S.C. § 7411(a)(1). The Agency carried out this mandate by promulgating NSPS to be specifically applied to designated source categories (e.g., iron and steel mills, pulp and paper plants, and electroplating facilities).

Parties who wish to construct major new air polluting sources in dirty air regions are also subject to a more stringent set of requirements, generically referred to as "New Source Review." These sources must first comply with technology-based standards based upon the "lowest achievable emission rate" ("LAER"), i.e., the most stringent achievable emission standard contained in the implementation plan of any state for the class or category of source in question, or any more stringent emission limitation that is achieved in practice for that source or category. Clean Air Act § 173(a)(2), 42 U.S.C. § 7503(a)(2) and Clean Air Act § 171(3), 42 U.S.C. § 7501(3).

Second, new and modified stationary sources in nonattainment areas must comply with "emission offset requirements," i.e., legally enforceable reductions from existing sources in the same nonattainment area above and beyond any reductions that would otherwise be required for those other sources. Clean Air Act § 173(a)(1)(A), 42 U.S.C. § 7503(a)(1)(A).

Third, the owner or operator of any proposed new or modified source within a nonattainment area must demonstrate that all major stationary sources it owns or operates in the same state are in compliance or on a schedule for compliance with all applicable Clean Air Act emission limitations and standards. Clean Air Act § 173(a)(3), 42 U.S.C. § 7503(a)(3). And finally, proposed new or modified nonattainment area source owners or operators must demonstrate that the benefits of their proposed source significantly outweigh the environmental and social costs imposed as a result of its location, construction, or modification. Clean Air Act § 173(a)(5), 42 U.S.C. § 7503(a)(5).

Proposals to approve new sources in nonattainment areas are sometimes challenged on the basis that the proposed offset emission reductions are contrary to the Act's requirements. *Citizens Against the Refinery's Effects, Inc. v. United States Environmental Protection Agency*, 643 F.2d 183 (4th Cir. 1981) was such a case. There a company wished to build a new refinery in a nonattainment area for ozone. It proposed to offset its hydrocarbon emissions by arranging with the Virginia Highway Department to decrease the Department's usage of a certain type of asphalt. The Virginia State Air Pollution Control Board approved this plan, as did EPA. In a challenge by a citizens group to the state and federal decisions that attempted to prevent the new refinery's construction, the Fourth Circuit rejected the plaintiff's arguments that EPA had used the wrong base year to compare usage of cutback asphalt, and that other aspects of its rationale for ratifying the state's approval of the new refinery had been arbitrary and capricious. The court reasoned that Congress had intended that the states and EPA be given flexibility in designing SIPs and the terms of permits, and that the governments' actions were neither arbitrary nor capricious. *Id.*

2. New Source Limitations in Attainment Areas

Major new or modified sources of criteria pollutants in (mainly rural) areas, where existing air quality is cleaner than the NAAQS, are also required to meet two sets of requirements: New Source Performance Standards (NSPS), as described above, and separate standards to prevent the "significant deterioration" of air quality ("PSD"). Beyond preventing adverse effects on public health, PSD rules are intended to promote economic growth in a manner consistent with preserving clean-air resources, and to protect air quality in and around national parks and other areas of natural or scenic value. Clean Air Act § 160, 42 U.S.C. § 7470.

PSD requirements apply to "major emitting facilities." This term is defined in the Act as a stationary source of any air pollutant(s) that appears on a statutory list of types of sources and emits (or has the potential to emit) 100 tons per year or more of a criteria pollutant. The term also includes any non-listed source with the potential to emit 250 tons per year or more of any air pollutant. Clean Air Act § 169(1), 42 U.S.C. § 7479(1).

Under the statute, states are required to classify their attainment areas into Classes I, II, or III, based on how pristine their outdoor air is measured to be. These classifications differ in the maximum amounts of air pollutant increases that are allowed in them. Class I areas, the cleanest, receive the strictest protections. Class III areas, where air quality is already more degraded, are permitted the highest maximum allowable increases in pollution. *See* Clean Air Act §§ 162 and 163(b), 42 U.S.C. §§ 7472 and 7473(b). The attainment area classifications may be re-designated by individual states, under limited conditions, as long as those states follow a specified procedure that includes an analysis of the impacts of re-designation, public hearings, consultation with federal land managers, and approval by EPA. Clean Air Act § 164, 42 U.S.C. § 7474.

Entities that wish to construct or modify major emitting facilities in attainment areas must meet several requirements to satisfy the statute. They must apply for "preconstruction permits" from EPA or state officials. They must also do a number of other things, including: (i) demonstrating that emissions from their proposed facility will not cause or contribute to air pollution in excess of the NAAQS or any maximum allowable pollutant concentration for the class of nonattainment area in which they are located, (ii) preparing an air quality impact analysis on any growth that will be associated with their proposed facility, (iii) showing that their facility will utilize the best available control technology ("BACT") for every regulated pollutant it will emit, and (iv) agreeing to conduct emissions self-monitoring to determine the impact of their facility's emissions on air quality. Clean Air Act § 165(1), 42 U.S.C. § 7475.

The statute generally defines BACT as "an emissions limitation based on the maximum degree of [pollutant] reduction ... which the permitting authority, on a case-by-case basis, taking into account energy, environmental, and economic impacts and other costs, determines is available for [the] facility." Clean Air Act § 169(1), 42 U.S.C. § 7479(1). In most instances, the "permitting authority" that makes case-by-case decisions as to what control measures constitute BACT is the state in which a new or modified facility in a clean air area is proposed. However, in an important decision, the U.S. Supreme Court has made clear that EPA has "supervisory authority" over the reasonableness of state permitting authorities' BACT determinations; and the Agency may issue a stop construction order if a BACT selection is not reasonable. *See Alaska Department of Environmental Conservation v. Environmental Protection Agency*, 540 U.S. 461 (2004).

D. Air Pollution Controls on Motor Vehicles

Motor vehicles emit a substantial proportion of several designated criteria pollutants. In recognition of the hazards posed by motor vehicle pollution, the Clean Air Act established standards limiting motor vehicle tailpipe emissions and regulating the contents of vehicle fuels and fuel additives.

The Act directed EPA to establish standards "applicable to the emission of any air pollutant from any class or classes of new motor vehicles or new motor vehicle engines, which in [EPA's] judgment cause, or contribute to, air pollution which may reasonably be anticipated to endanger public health or welfare." Clean Air Act § 202(a)(1), 42 U.S.C. § 7521(a)(1). EPA's new vehicle standards were required to "reflect the greatest degree of emission reduction achievable through the application of available technology . . . giving appropriate consideration to cost, energy, and safety factors associated with the application of such technology." Clean Air Act § 202(a)(3)(A)(i), 42 U.S.C. § 7521(a)(3)(A)(i). These standards must apply during the "useful life" of a vehicle, as defined in the statute. Clean Air Act § 202(a)(1), 42 U.S.C. § 7421(a)(1). EPA adhered to Congress' mandate. It promulgated separate sets of emission standards for light-duty passenger vehicles, light-duty trucks, motorcycles, and heavy-duty trucks. *See* 40 C.F.R. pt. 86. It also banned lead additives in gasoline, a measure that has been credited with the immense improvement in public health, particularly among children.

The Clean Air Act generally preempts state regulation of motor vehicle emissions. Clean Air Act § 209(a)(1), 42 U.S.C. § 7543. However, Congress created a special exception for the State of California because its state laws already regulated mobile sources prior to passage of the federal statute. Clean Air Act § 209(b), 42 U.S.C. § 7543(b). California is permitted to set its own vehicle standards up to two years before the commencement of any vehicle model year, and all other states may adopt standards of their own as long as they are identical to those adopted in California. Clean Air Act § 177, 42 U.S.C. § 7507.

EPA is also required to conduct a testing program on samples of new cars that must be provided by the manufacturer. Vehicles that pass Agency testing receive a "certificate of conformity," which is legally required before any motor vehicle may be sold in the United States. Clean Air Act § 206, 42 U.S.C. § 7525. Parties who sell vehicles without a certificate of conformity are subject to steep civil penalties. The Act also creates penalties for persons who "remove or render inoperative" any automobile pollution control device, or who knowingly manufacture or sell any part or component that will "bypass, defeat or render inoperative" a vehicle pollution control device. Clean Air Act §§ 203(a)(3)(A) and (B), 42 U.S.C. §§ 7522(a)(3)(A) and (B).

Checkpoints

- The common law doctrines of nuisance and trespass have retained vitality as sources of law regarding air pollution problems.
- Courts vary in the approaches they have taken with respect to the remedy to be awarded successful plaintiffs in common law air pollution nuisance cases.
- "Criteria pollutants" are air pollutants from different sources that may reasonably be expected to endanger public health or welfare.
- The Clean Air Act requires EPA to identify criteria pollutants and to prepare "air quality criteria" documents for each identified criteria pollutant that indicate the effects on public health and welfare of those pollutants and techniques available to control their emission.
- EPA must also establish National Ambient Air Quality Standards for each criteria pollutant reflecting the level of air purity necessary to protect the public health (with an adequate margin of safety) and the public welfare. Areas that have air cleaner than the standards required are deemed "attainment areas." Dirtier air regions are known as "nonattainment areas."
- Considerations of economic costs may play no part in the setting of health-based National Ambient Air Quality Standards.
- Individual states are required to adopt State Implementation Plans containing enforceable emissions limitations that will result in the implementation and maintenance of National Ambient Air Quality Standards.
- State Implementation Plans must be submitted to EPA for review. Where the federal agency determines that a state's plan is inconsistent with the Act, EPA may create a binding Federal Implementation Plan for the control of criteria pollutants in the state.
- The Clean Air Act is technology-forcing legislation, i.e., legislation designed to force regulated entities to develop and use new pollution control devices and techniques where such techniques are not technically or economically feasible.
- The current Clean Air Act contains an extensive list of hazardous air pollutants.
- EPA is required to publish a listing of all categories and subcategories of major sources of all listed hazardous air pollutants and to develop maximum available control technology standards for those sources.
- New and modified sources of air pollutants in nonattainment areas must meet New Source Performance Standards (requiring the use of best demonstrated control technology in each source category) and New Source Review (mandating use of air pollution control technology that will achieve the "lowest achievable emission rate" and "offsets" to any new pollution those new or modified sources will create through reductions of pollutant emissions from existing sources).

- In attainment areas, new or modified sources must meet both New Source Performance Standards and Prevention of Significant Deterioration Standards.
- Under Prevention of Significant Deterioration requirements, states are required to classify their attainment areas based on how clean their air is.
- Entities that wish to construct new or modified sources in attainment areas must obtain preconstruction permits requiring, among other things, the use of the best available control technology.
- As directed by Congress, EPA has created new motor vehicle emissions standards that reflect the greatest degree of emission reduction achievable throughout the useful life of the vehicle.
- EPA is required to test samples of new cars, which must be supplied by auto manufacturers, for compliance with applicable standards.
- Passing EPA's tests is a prerequisite to obtain the "Certificate of Conformity" that is required before a vehicle may legally be sold in the United States.

Chapter 3

Climate Change Law

Roadmap

- Grasp how international commitments and laws affect legal obligations to reduce greenhouse gas emissions as well as account for climate change in the United States, in other nations, and under international law.
- Understand how the federal Clean Air Act may require operators of facilities to reduce their emissions of greenhouse gases.
- Identify how other federal laws, such as the Clean Water Act and the Endangered Species Act, require actions by the federal government and private persons to respond to climate change effects.
- Learn how tort lawsuits have sought—and many instances failed—to impose liability for climate change damages on large emitters of greenhouse gases, and how future lawsuits might succeed.
- Understand how state environmental laws have approached climate change issues, and how these state and local approaches differ from federal approaches.

Vast quantities of greenhouse gases, such as carbon dioxide and methane, emitted by human activities have already begun to affect the global environment. According to the overwhelming consensus among climatologists and other scientists, concentrations of carbon dioxide in the ambient atmosphere have nearly doubled since the beginning of the Industrial Revolution, and those emissions have already caused global surface temperatures to increase by 0.8 degrees C. These temperature increases will likely continue because greenhouse gases (in particular, carbon dioxide) persist in the atmosphere once they are emitted, and—if current emissions of greenhouse gases from human activities do not abate—global surface temperatures will likely exceed 2.0 degrees C by the year 2100. This temperature rise can significantly disrupt global climate systems and weather patterns, cause sea level rise that will drown low-lying coast areas and islands, and lead to such severe weather events as heat waves, droughts, floods, and destructive storms.

Because of its threat of damage and disruption on a global scale, climate change is one of the most serious and difficult challenges for international and U.S. environmental laws. Greenhouse gas emissions arise from an enormous array of human activities, including the combustion of fossil fuels for energy; and most greenhouse gas emissions from any location on the planet contribute equally to climate change effects. Because greenhouse gases such as carbon dioxide can remain in the atmosphere for centuries, the accumulated greenhouse gases already in the atmosphere have resulted from past activities by developed nations who benefited from those economic activities. Their requests for developing nations now to restrict emissions from their economic activities spark concerns about fairness, the need for equal economic opportunity, and self-determination.

As a result, attempts to control greenhouse gas emissions at any level have caused political conflict at the international level. Many nations either disagree with each other on the best ways to reduce climate change risks or cannot reach agreements even within themselves on how to control their own emissions. In the United States, for example, attempts to create federal legislation to set limits on greenhouse gas emissions have largely failed, and successive presidential administrations have sharply changed course on greenhouse gas control priorities every eight years since 1992.

This impasse has caused climate change law in the United States to grow by amalgamation. Rather than being grounded in an integrated statute setting out a single coherent strategy to reduce emissions, federal efforts have relied on a complex mixture of binding and voluntary international commitments, extension of existing federal laws and regulations crafted originally for different purposes, and state and local programs to promote clean energy and greenhouse gas reductions.

This chapter summarizes some of the most important features of the complex legal landscape governing climate change responses. It describes the most important provisions of relevant international treaties, the federal Clean Air Act and other federal environmental statutes, and key state environmental and energy laws. This chapter also gives an overview of the ways that tort claims have sought recovery from greenhouse gas emitters or to force governmental action to control emissions. Last, it focuses on how non-environmental statutes and regulations—such as disclosure requirements for sales of securities in publicly traded corporations—may have important consequences for climate change controls.

I. International Climate Change Treaties and Their Legal Effects within the United States

After scientists initially identified climate change effects as a serious global concern in the late 1970s, a series of international treaties and conventions has tried different strategies to encourage reductions in greenhouse gas emissions. These types of controls are typically referred to as *mitigation*. By contrast, attempts to prepare for unavoidable climate change effects through planning and strengthening infrastructure is called *adaptation*.

Climate change law typically strives to achieve both aims, and international treaties have sought to promote aggressive mitigation measures by current emitters in tandem with heightened efforts to assist nations (particularly developing ones) to prepare and implement adaptation strategies. These adaptation efforts have typically consisted of direct financial support, transfer of needed technologies, and promotion of systems to pay for transferable emission reduction credits.

A. International Legal Commitments by the United States on Climate Change

The array of international laws and conventions governing or affecting climate change is vast and bewildering. The United States has played a key role in the negotiation and creation of numerous international conferences and instruments on climate change, but it has endorsed aspirational goals and strategic planning rather than binding international agreements that would commit it to concrete emission reductions. Against this backdrop, three international climate conventions matter for charting legal obligations in the United States: the United Nations Framework Convention on Climate Change (UNFCCC), the Paris Agreement, and customary international laws created by the conduct of nations under a sense of legal obligation. This section briefly explores each agreement, and it points out numerous other international agreements on other topics that might affect legal climate obligations in the United States (e.g., the U.N. Convention on the Law of the Sea).

1. UNFCCC

The UNFCCC is the keystone environmental convention that supports and structures international efforts to work on mitigating, adapting to, and forestalling climate change. After the United Nations opened the UNFCCC for signatures in 1992, it quickly obtained the support of enough nations to enter into force in 1992. The UNFCCC now has more than 192 signatories—including the United States—and has become one of the most widely adopted international agreements in history. President George H.W. Bush signed the Convention, and the U.S. Senate ratified it in 1992.

As a framework convention, the UNFCCC essentially sets the stage for future negotiations and agreements. It imposes relatively few substantive obligations on its signatories, but those commitments play a large role in guiding and spurring international climate negotiations and activities within its overarching structure. The UNFCCC's key legal commitments by ratifying countries include: (i) stabilizing greenhouse gas concentrations in the atmosphere at levels that would prevent dangerous anthropogenic climate change; (ii) submitting data on their greenhouse gas emissions broken down by sources and sinks; (iii) fostering the conservation and enhancement of natural sinks of greenhouse gases, such as forests and other terrestrial ecosystems; and (iv) cooperating to adapt to climate change impacts such as natural disasters and sea level rise.

The signatories, or Parties, to the UNFCCC meet annually at the Conference of the Parties (COP) to review progress under the UNFCCC and negotiate additional agreements to implement their UNFCCC commitments. For example, one COP—in Kyoto in 1997—led to an additional international agreement that imposed binding emission limits on its signatories. This Kyoto Protocol served as an important initial attempt to translate the UNFCCC's aspirational goals and diffuse framework into enforcement and specific legal obligations. Notably, the United States signed but never ratified the Kyoto Protocol, and the agreement has now largely expired. The Kyoto Protocol's initial creation of mechanisms to track, trade, and structure varying commitments by its Parties to reduce their emissions, however, has strongly influenced subsequent international agreements and national emission trading systems.

2. *The Paris Agreement*

In addition to the UNFCCC, the United States has entered into the Paris Agreement. This agreement is the latest, and most important, agreement reached under the UNFCCC, and nearly every nation on earth has agreed to its terms since its promulgation in December 2015. Notably, the United States agreed to join the Paris Agreement as an executive agreement under the previously ratified UNFCCC (which sidestepped the need for Senate ratification of the Paris Agreement), but its continued participation has fallen into doubt after President Donald Trump's announced intent to withdraw the United States from the agreement.

The Paris Agreement intentionally uses a broad and flexible "ground-up" approach that allows each nation to determine its contribution to emissions reductions and the methods it will use to achieve them. The agreement's most important element is its requirement for Nationally Determined Contributions (NDCs), which allow each nation to set its own targets and actions within its own political system. Each nation submits a revised NDC at least once every five years, Art. 4(9), and each successive submission should identify more ambitious reductions in emissions. The NDCs are reviewed and revised every five years, and collectively they should describe expected emission reductions to achieve the Paris Agreement's aspirational goal of limiting temperature increases to 1.5 degrees C. The agreement then combines the NDC process with important additional tools, including transparency mandates (such as domestic monitoring, reporting, and verification), allowance for linkage and coordination of international policies (including carbon trading through "internationally transferred mitigation outcomes"), and opportunities for financial assistance and determinations of loss and damage.

While the Paris Agreement has garnered praise as one of the most ambitious international agreements in history, with virtually universal participation by almost every nation, its potential for application within the United States seems paltry at best. Most notably, President Trump has announced his intention to withdraw the United States from the agreement. While this withdrawal cannot take effect under the Paris Agreement's terms until 2020, Art. 28(1), it leaves the United States in the dubious position as the sole signatory to the UNFCCC (indeed, the world community of nations) that has chosen not to participate in the agreement. In addition, the Paris Agreement by its own terms allows each nation to determine its contribution to emission reductions under its own laws. As a result, the Agreement does not impose any new obligations that would translate into self-ratifying obligations effective under U.S. law. Nonetheless, any U.S. citizens or corporations operating in other nations would need to account for the domestic laws that each nation may implement to satisfy its obligations under the Paris Agreement or the UNFCCC.

3. *Customary International Laws and Other Subject-Specific International Commitments*

Beyond the two international agreements, international law may apply to U.S. actors in other ways. For example, international law can arise outside of treaties through the creation of customary international law. This type of law results from the combination of consistent patterns of practice by nations undertaken with a sense of legal obligation (*opinio juris*). The United States has incorporated customary international law into federal common law as a matter of long-standing precedent from the U.S. Supreme Court. *In re Paquette Habana,* 175 U.S. 677 (1900); *In re Charming Betsy,* 16 U.S. 64 (1804). If nations begin to act in consistent fashion in the international arena to avoid harming the global climate under a clear sense of legal obligation, they may create a norm of international law that could create legal obligations for the United States and its citizens.

This prospect, however, faces several hurdles. As a matter of principle, customary international law applies almost solely to sovereigns and their instrumentalities. It generally will not directly apply to individuals or corporations except for rare instances of universal norms (such as crimes under international law) or when nations pass domestic laws to implement customary international law. Nations can also prevent the formation of customary international law norms that apply to their actions by expressly disavowing consent to those emerging legal precepts and consistently acting in ways that reject the customary law principle. To date, the United States has not expressly consented to the creation or application of customary international law norms pertaining to climate change that would apply to its actions (beyond its express commitments under international agreements). In addition, U.S. statutes would override any international customary norms as a matter of sovereignty under any U.S. federal law governing a domestic legal proceeding (even if that preemption constituted a separate violation of international law that would create state responsibility for the United States itself).

International law may also invoke climate change obligations, but under a different cloak. If an international treaty or convention imposes substantive obligations on its Parties that require supplemental responses to address new conditions caused by climate change, a signatory may find itself bound by international law norms to act on climate change to satisfy its existing commitments for other purposes. For example, climate change already subjects rare and threatened species to additional stress, and it will undeniably contribute substantially to an accelerated loss of biodiversity and crucial habitat. Nations that have joined the Convention on Biological Diversity, as a result, may find themselves obligated to take additional steps to mitigate or adapt to climate change as necessary to protect biodiversity per their commitments under the Convention. Members to the U.N. Convention on the Law of the Sea may find themselves in a similar legal posture. Notably, however, the United States has not joined or ratified either of these international agreements, but it participates in other agreements where climate change effects may bolster or create additional dimensions to existing U.S. obligations. For example, the United States has joined the Montreal Protocol to the Vienna Convention on the Control of Ozone Depleting Substances. Several ozone-harming chemicals have strong greenhouse gas effects, and the United States may find itself taking steps to control their production and distribution as part of its international legal commitment to protect the stratospheric ozone layer.

II. U.S. Laws That Apply to Climate Change

There is no comprehensive federal climate change statute in the United States. Congress made its last (failed) attempt to pass comprehensive climate change legislation through the proposed American Climate and Energy Security Act in 2008, and the current Trump Administration has made clear its intention not to consider climate change as a significant priority. As a result, legal obligations on climate change in the United States rely on a welter of older federal environmental and energy laws written for other purposes, as well as varying state and local laws.

A. Clean Air Act Requirements

The primary federal environmental statute invoked to address climate change is the federal Clean Air Act. This statute, which Congress has not significantly revised since 1990, does not expressly direct EPA to regulate greenhouse gas emissions as a form of air pollution that requires permitting or controls. The statute's broad definitions of "air pollutant" and its sweeping mandate to EPA have nonetheless sparked attempts from 2008 through 2016 to use several of its programs to restrict greenhouse gas emissions and counteract climate change effects. These initiatives, however, remain in a state of legal flux in light of efforts in the past two years to either revoke the new climate change regulations, suspend enforcement of their requirements, or alter interpretations of the Clean Air Act to narrow its applicability to climate change concerns.

1. *Authority to Regulate Greenhouse Gas Emissions as Air Pollution under the Clean Air Act*

To regulate greenhouse gas emissions under the Clean Air Act, EPA first had to overcome objections that Congress did not intend for the statute to apply to greenhouse gas emissions. According to critics, the Clean Air Act targeted only conventional pollutants that degraded air quality in a relatively local area that directly injured public health. Greenhouse gases, under this interpretation, did not qualify because they mix quickly into ambient air and affect global concentration levels rather than local air quality conditions, and they only injure public health indirectly by altering climate conditions to exacerbate floods, storms, heat waves, diseases, and other threats.

The U.S. Supreme Court decisively rejected this argument in its landmark *Massachusetts v. EPA* opinion, 549 U.S. 497, in 2007. When EPA denied a rulemaking petition to regulate greenhouse gases from motor vehicles by disclaiming any authority under the Clean Air Act to regulate greenhouse gases (and declining to exercise that authority even if it had it), the Court disagreed. It ruled instead that greenhouse gases comfortably fell within the Clean Air Act's broad definition of "air pollutant," and the Court further ruled that EPA could regulate them if it determined that they caused or contributed to climate change. Rather than mandate EPA to regulate greenhouse gases under the Clean Air Act, the Court instead remanded the case back to EPA to decide whether greenhouse gases, as pollutants, caused or contributed to air pollution that endangered public health or welfare—i.e., an "endangerment finding." It expressly forbade EPA, however, from refusing to regulate greenhouse gas emissions on any other grounds of expediency, cost, difficulty, or deference on foreign affairs concerns.

The regulatory dominoes fell quickly after *Massachusetts v. EPA*, aided by the election of President Barack Obama in 2008. EPA issued its endangerment finding in 2009, and that determination triggered a series of statutory obligations for EPA to issue rules to address the threat under the Clean Air Act's programs for mobile sources, large stationary sources that emit regulated pollutants, and certain new and existing facilities. EPA quickly followed up with a host of regulations to require reporting of greenhouse gas emissions, establish permitting obligations, and include climate change effects under other programs (including a rule specifically to govern emissions from light-duty motor vehicles in 2010). The most notable regulatory restrictions arose under its programs for Prevention of Significant Deterioration permits (PSD) and New Source Performance Standards/Existing Source Performance Standards (NSPS/ESPS).

2. PSD Permitting for Major Greenhouse Gas Sources

The Clean Air Act requires that major facilities constructed in areas where the air meets national ambient air quality standards must first obtain a PSD permit before they begin construction. EPA attempted to extend the PSD program by requiring large facilities that emit greenhouse gases to obtain permits limiting their emissions of those gases. This initiative required a series of rulemakings to establish the triggers, timetables, and thresholds for the permit program, which culminated in EPA's Tailoring Rule. This rule set out a series of emission thresholds that would trigger an obligation to obtain a permit depending on whether the facility emitted other pollutants in addition to greenhouse gases or was a minor source that emitted a relatively small amount of greenhouse gases. The Tailoring Rule spurred a wave of litigation to challenge several key aspects of the rule, including its abandonment of statutory emission threshold triggers and its assertion of authority to regulate facilities that emitted solely greenhouse gases.

The U.S. Supreme Court resolved those challenges in *Utility Air Regulatory Group v. EPA*, 134 S. Ct. 2427 (2014). The Court struck down EPA's attempts to regulate carbon dioxide and other greenhouse gases as an air pollutant for purposes of the PSD program by finding that EPA's attempt to include them conflicted with other express requirements of the Clean Air Act (e.g., low emission thresholds to trigger permit obligations). Nonetheless, EPA received an important practical win when the Court upheld EPA's authority under the Clean Air Act to require greenhouse gas controls as an element in selecting the Best Available Control Technologies for a particular facility. This ruling allowed EPA to potentially include greenhouse gas emission restrictions for large sources that emit more than 80 percent of the United States' current greenhouse gas emissions.

3. *NSPS/ESPS Requirements for Greenhouse Gases and the Fate of the Clean Power Plan*

In addition to extending the PSD program to cover large greenhouse gas emitters, EPA promulgated new emission requirements for facilities that fell under its New Source Performance Standard [NSPS] and Existing Source Performance Standard [ESPS] programs. Beyond requiring permits under the PSD rules for emissions of criteria pollutants that affect the quality of ambient air surrounding a facility, the Clean Air Act also requires facilities in certain industrial categories to meet technology-driven emission standards for regulated pollutants they emit. These NSPS standards can reach a broader set of pollutants, and they can apply uniformly to an industrial sector without regard to their location or whether the facility lies within an area that does not attain national ambient air quality standards. In addition, if EPA has not yet regulated emissions of a particular pollutant, it can impose similar emission restrictions on existing facilities in the same industrial sector. To do so, EPA must specify reductions in pollutants that a particular technology designated as the Best System of Emission Reduction (BSER) can reach, and then require facilities to attain those levels (even if they choose a different technology).

EPA sought to extend the NSPS and ESPS programs to fossil-fueled power plants and regulate their emissions of greenhouse gases. This regulatory program, called the Clean Power Plan, emerged after years of hotly contested rulemaking proceedings and public hearings at EPA, and it would have imposed a novel and sweeping set of standards to reduce power sector emissions. For example, the Clean Power Plan would have allowed power generators to attain low emission standards by participating in market trading mechanisms or modulating the amount of power demanded by their consumers. It would have also forced facilities to improve the efficiency of their combustion processes in ways that would reduce their emissions of greenhouse gases.

As one of the crowning achievements of the Obama Administration's climate action plan, the Clean Power Plan became the immediate target of vigorous opposition and litigation. The U.S. Supreme Court again stepped in by issuing a stay that prevented EPA from implementing or enforcing the Clean Power Plan's requirements until the Court had completed its review and ruling on challenges to the rule.

The Trump Administration subsequently proposed a substitute for the Clean Power Plan, labeled the "Affordable Clean Energy Rule," that would only allow power plants to cut back on greenhouse gas emissions by adopting on-site ("inside the fenceline") measures to encourage plant operating efficiency. This preliminary proposal would also allow individual states to set their own emissions standards for highly polluting facilities. At best, the direct result of this plan would likely be a minimal decrease in greenhouse gas emissions from power plants. It is not clear at this writing whether the Trump administration will modify its initial proposal significantly. Nor can it be predicted with certainty whether whatever final regulation EPA adopts will survive judicial review. This situation has created a sort of limbo for electric utility companies that are faced with uncertainty as to which emissions limitations they will ultimately be required to follow at power plants that presently burn fossil fuels.

B. Other Federal Environmental Statutes That Create Climate Change Legal Obligations

Given its broad swath of effects on the environment, climate change unsurprisingly raises new and difficult challenges under other federal and state environmental laws in addition to the Clean Air Act. For example, the federal Clean Water Act requires permits for all discharges of pollutants into waters of the United States to assure those discharges undergo treatment (if needed) to meet appropriate technological standards. Other portions of the Clean Water

Act require permits for actions that discharge or fill wetlands that qualify as waters of the United States. These programs will need to wrestle with climate change's effect on the amount and locations of waters of the United States (as storms become more severe and unpredictable, or shifts in rainfall patterns create droughts and sculpt new watersheds), alteration of the quality of water (as water levels drop, their capacity to absorb pollutants may change), and preparation for potential spills of pollutants into those waters. For example, some lawsuits have contended that operators of facilities abutting waterways failed to account for climate change effects that raise the risks of spills and environmental damages when they prepared their spill prevention and contingency plans. *Conservation Law Foundation v. Exxon Mobil Corp.*, Complaint, Civ. No. 1:16-cv-11950 (MLW) (D. Mass. filed Sept. 29, 2016).

Other federal environmental permitting programs have also struggled to account for climate change. The Endangered Species Act, for example, requires the Secretary of either the Department of Interior (for non-marine species) or the Department of Commerce (for marine species) to identify species that are either threatened or endangered by extinction. In making these selections, the agencies must forecast which species will face mortal threats from climate change over relatively long periods (say, 50 years) and decide whether to classify them as threatened now because of a high risk of extinction 50 to 100 years in the future. Attempts by the United States to list such species as protected under the Endangered Species Act—such as the polar bear or bearded walrus—have triggered a firestorm of controversy and litigation. Some environmental advocacy groups have invoked the Endangered Species Act to oppose the issuance of federal permits or federal actions that they contend will jeopardize a protected species, including the permitting of fossil-fueled power plants that arguably would contribute to climate change.

Efforts to force federal action on climate change through these other federal environmental statutes, however, have yielded inconsistent results. Neither the Clean Water Act nor the Endangered Species Act have spurred comprehensive or vigorous federal environmental responses to climate change at this time. For example, when environmental groups filed a petition for rulemaking to force EPA to act under the Clean Water Act to treat ocean acidification as an impairment of marine waters of the United States, EPA only responded by issuing a broad framework policy for further research. Notice of Voluntary Dismissal, *Center for Biological Diversity v. EPA*, Case No. 2:09-cv-00670 (JCC) (settlement agreement filed on March 11, 2010); Memorandum from D. Keehner, Director of EPA Office of Wetlands, Oceans and Watersheds, to Water Divisions Directors, Re: *Integrated Reporting and Listing Decisions Related to Ocean Acidification* (Nov. 15, 2010). Similarly,

EPA has rejected efforts to invoke the Endangered Species Act to stop federal environmental permits for fossil-fueled power generation plants that would contribute to global climate change effects. *See, e.g.*, Memorandum from U.S. Fish & Wildlife Service Director to Regional Directors, Re: *Expectations for Consultations on Actions that Would Emit Greenhouse Gases* (May 14, 2008); Letter from R. Meyers, EPA Office of Air and Radiation, to D. Hall and J. Lecky, Re: *Endangered Species Act and GHG Emitting Activities*, Oct. 3, 2008 (concluding that any greenhouse gas emissions from any single coal-fired power plant outside Alaska would have too small an effect on global climate change to require permits under the Endangered Species Act for the incidental taking of polar bears).

At least one federal environmental statute (outside of the Clean Air Act) has had a substantial impact on climate change policy and legal obligations: the National Environmental Policy Act (NEPA). NEPA requires the federal government to assess the impacts of major federal actions that may have a significant impact on the environment (as we discuss in Chapter 8). Specifically, when a federal agency wishes to undertake a major action (such as issuing a federal permit needed to build a new power plant or pipeline), it must first conduct an environmental assessment to weigh the project's potential impact on the environment. If the project has little or no impact, the agency can issue a finding of no significant impact and then grant the permit. If the project does impact the environment, however, the agency usually must prepare a full environmental impact statement (EIS). An EIS can be an intense and time-consuming endeavor, and failure to follow NEPA's procedures may lead to a preliminary injunction to halt activity and a suspension or rescission of the underlying project. Interestingly, NEPA requires only a careful evaluation of the environmental impacts, but doesn't impose a substantive standard—an agency can proceed with an environmentally harmful project under NEPA, as long as it has carefully considered those consequences.

Given the statute's sweeping scope and powerful remedies, NEPA has understandably emerged as one of the favorite legal grounds to challenge projects that emit greenhouse gases or fail to account for climate change impacts. For example, during the first five months of 2018 environmental groups had already filed at least 10 NEPA challenges to federal agency actions based on climate change concerns. These cases have scored notable successes. For example, in *Center for Biological Diversity v. National Highway Transportation Administration*, 508 F.2d 508 (9th Cir. 2007), *opinion vacated and withdrawn*, 538 F.3d 117 (9th Cir. 2008), the Ninth Circuit rejected the agency's issuance of a fuel efficiency standard that would only slightly reduce greenhouse gas emissions from vehicles because the agency's environmental assessment failed to monetize the cost of carbon emissions or to provide particularized efficiency standards for certain high-emitting vehicles. More recently, the federal district court of Montana reached a similar conclusion in *Montana Environmental Information Center v. U.S. Office of Surface Mining*, No. CV-106-M-DWN (D. Montana, Aug. 14, 2017) by holding that the U.S. Office of Surface Mining had improperly failed to account for the indirect costs of carbon emissions in its Finding of No Significant Impact for a proposed expansion of a coal mine on federal land. Similar NEPA challenges have also arisen against liquefied natural gas plants, *Sierra Club v. U.S. Department of Energy*, 867 F.3d 189 (D.C. Cir. 2017); and environmental advocates will undoubtedly continue to rely on NEPA as a mechanism to force federal planning and action to deal with climate change.

Continuing NEPA litigation over federal actions involving climate change is likely to take place against a backdrop of confusion and retrenchment in federal agency guidance sparked by the recent change in climate policy under the Trump Administration. In particular, the federal Council on Environmental Quality (CEQ) issued its final guidance on NEPA reviews of greenhouse gas emissions and climate change in mid-2016. Memorandum from C. Goldfuss to Heads of Federal Departments and Agencies, Re: *Final Guidance for Federal Departments and Agencies on Consideration of Greenhouse Gas Emissions and the Effects of Climate Change in National Environmental Policy Act Reviews* (Aug. 1, 2016). This guidance, in fact, simply made official the informal direction that CEQ had provided since 2014 on how to account for greenhouse gas emission impacts. President Trump, however, directed the withdrawal of the CEQ guidance within a few months of taking office, Executive Order 13783 (March 28, 2017), and CEQ has retracted the guidance. 82 Fed. Reg. 16,576 (April 5, 2017). To the extent that federal climate change policy continues to rely on agency guidances, memoranda, and executive orders rather than statutory directives or formal agency regulations, it seems likely to continue to swing erratically and widely in response to the immediate results of contested federal elections.

C. State Laws and Regulations

Given the inconstant nature of federal climate policy and the litigation uncertainties swirling around it, state and local governments have taken their own steps to fill the void. These actions have taken two forms. First, several state governments have created their own regional affiliations and organizations to coordinate climate change initiatives and policies, including the trading of greenhouse gas emissions across state borders. Second, several large states have enacted their own state laws and regulations to control greenhouse gas emissions within their borders.

The most notable regional programs stretch from the eastern United States—where the Regional Greenhouse Gas Initiative (RGGI) includes several states along the East Coast—through the Midwestern Greenhouse Gas Accord outward to the Western Climate Initiative's coordination of emissions among several West Coast states and Canadian provincial governments. Following the withdrawal of several western states, however, California is the only U.S. state remaining in the Western Climate Initiative.

RGGI brought together nine states in an emissions trading program that focuses exclusively on fossil-fueled power generators. Pursuant to a nonbinding memorandum of understanding, participating states agreed to coordinate their emissions reduction requirements by establishing a regional cap-and-trade system that required power plants to buy credits that would allow them to emit greenhouse gases. The states in RGGI have seen substantial reductions in greenhouse gas emissions—although some critics claim that other factors caused the reductions—and the program has generated substantial revenues for participating states. Nevertheless, the stability and effectiveness of these regional approaches depends in part on the vicissitudes of state elections and leadership changes that may cause states to enter, or withdraw, from the coalitions.

On a more local level, some states have shouldered the burden of regulating greenhouse gases within their borders by imposing their own direct state laws or regulatory standards. The most aggressive state on greenhouse gas policies is California, which has passed its own climate change policy statute. The California Global Warming Securities Act (also known as AB 32) sets up a state-wide cap-and-trade system for greenhouse gas emissions that includes all industrial sectors, including transportation. AB 32 will require large greenhouse gas emitters in California, including fossil-fueled power plants, to obtain either permits or allowances to control their emissions. California has also invoked its waiver authority under the federal Clean Air Act to require more stringent emission limits on mobile source vehicles sold within the state (although, at the time of this writing, EPA had yet to approve California's most recent request for a waiver). Beyond California, other states (e.g., Washington State) have included limits on greenhouse gas emissions in their state air quality permit programs, and some states have indirectly reduced greenhouse gas emissions through requiring utilities to generate a set amount or percentage of their power from renewable or low-carbon sources. All of these state programs, however, must operate within limits imposed by the federal Constitution's dormant commerce clause provisions, which prohibit efforts by states to explicitly disfavor commerce in other states or improperly burden interstate commerce in favor of its local producers. *Rocky Mountain Farmer's Union v. Corey,* 730 F.3d 1070 (9th Cir. 2013).

D. Tort Liability

Like federal regulations and policy, climate change tort litigation in U.S. courts has seen dramatic gains and reversals of direction. A wave of new court actions, however, foreshadows much more aggressive climate change litigation over the next several years.

The initial wave of climate tort actions consisted primarily of three keystone cases. Each of the cases brought slightly different plaintiffs and claims. In *Connecticut v. American Electric Power,* 564 U.S. 410 (2011), several state attorneys general brought a public nuisance action against utilities whose coal-fired power plants released enormous amounts of greenhouse gases, while *Comer v. Murphy Oil Company,* 607 F.3d 1049 (5th Cir. 2009) saw a class action suit by Mississippi residents who claimed that greenhouse gas emissions by a motley collection of energy, chemical, and other industrial defendants worsened the damage caused by Hurricane Katrina. *Kivalina v. Exxon Mobil,* by contrast, rested on claims by an Inuit village government that the defendants' greenhouse gas emissions had aggravated winter storms and weakened pack ice to a degree that they needed to relocate the village. The plaintiffs simply wanted the energy and chemical defendants to reimburse them for their relocation expenses.

Despite their differences, all three claims shared important features. First, the plaintiffs in all three actions filed their lawsuits in federal court. Second, all three actions sought recovery under federal common law tort theories, including public nuisance, trespass, nuisance, and negligence. While the plaintiffs also brought tort claims under state law, they urged the federal court to hear their state law claims under the court's supplemental jurisdiction, which authorizes courts to hear state claims arising from the same core operative facts underlying the federal action. It is important to note that the federal courts typically have discretion on whether to hear such supplemental claims.

The U.S. Supreme Court brought a conclusive end to this first wave of climate tort litigation in *Connecticut v. American Electric Power Co.* in 2011. In a unanimous opinion by Justice Ginsburg, the Court held that the federal Clean Air Act displaced any federal common law tort actions for damages arising from climate change. In its opinion, the Court emphasized that the displacement occurred when Congress passed the Clean Air Act and gave EPA thc power to regulate greenhouse gas emissions even if EPA never chose to exercise that power. As a result, EPA's reluctance to regulate greenhouse gases did not leave any room for the plaintiffs to bring their tort claims. After the ruling, each district court on remand dismissed both the federal tort claim and the associated state tort claims by refusing to exercise their supplemental jurisdiction.

After a hiatus of nearly a decade, climate tort actions returned in a new guise in 2017. Rather than suing under federal common law, several cities and local governments in California, New York, Washington State, Rhode Island, Maryland, and Colorado filed separate tort actions under their state laws to recover damages for harms caused by climate change. These lawsuits, filed in both state courts and federal courts (under diversity jurisdiction), seek compensation for climate change effects attributable to the defendants' emissions and false representations during their marketing and distribution of fossil fuel products. As this chapter is written, the cases have already yielded conflicting decisions on motions to dismiss and to remand the actions. Nonetheless, this area is likely to develop into a fast-moving and hotly contested branch of climate change law.

Finally, an entirely new form of climate litigation has begun to emerge. Under the long-standing public trust doctrine, governments bear a fiduciary duty to preserve certain resources that fall within the sovereignty of the public at large. In the past, this doctrine has primarily applied to certain limited categories of land, such as submerged river bottoms or coastal lands, and the courts have generally upheld restrictions on the state's ability to alienate those resources for private gain or to allow damage or waste to those public resources.

However, a set of underage minor plaintiffs have now invoked the public trust doctrine to claim that the federal and state governments have failed to meet their obligations to protect a new category of resource—the atmosphere. While virtually every action brought under state laws or regulations has failed, one set of plaintiffs, alleging violations of the federal public trust doctrine in federal district court, has survived dismissal motions and appear poised to proceed to trial. If the claim yields a concrete judgment that requires more aggressive action by the federal government, this breed of litigation may quickly become much more vigorous and common.

Checkpoints

- While the United States does not have a federal climate change statute, it uses a collection of other international, federal, and state environmental laws to require tracking, reporting, and control of greenhouse gas emissions.
- The United States has announced its desire to withdraw from the Paris Agreement, which is currently the leading international agreement for climate change actions by the international community.
    - The United States, however, remains a signatory to the U.N. Framework Convention on Climate Change, and it remains a member of the Paris Agreement under its terms until 2020.
    - The Paris Agreement does not impose any substantive emissions limits itself, and the United States can choose how it wishes to satisfy its general commitments under the Agreement.
- Although the U.S. Supreme Court has held that greenhouse gases are "pollutants" subject to regulation under the federal Clean Air Act, the Court struck down EPA's attempt to require permits for facilities that emit only greenhouse gases.
    - The Court has also stayed EPA's Clean Power Plan regulations, which would have limited emissions of greenhouse gases from fossil-fueled power plants under the Clean Air Act's performance standard program for new and existing sources.
    - It remains unclear the extent to which EPA can, or will, regulate greenhouse gases from facilities that also emit other regulated pollutants.
- As a result of recent electoral outcomes, the federal government has suspended or withdrawn several regulatory initiatives to regulate greenhouse gas emissions. These efforts include a proposal to formally overturn the Clean Power Plan regulations, a withdrawal of guidances and memoranda on the social cost of carbon emissions, and ways to account for greenhouse gas emissions in environmental impact statements.
- Other federal environmental statutes, including the Endangered Species Act and the Clean Water Act, may have limited applicability in requiring actions to mitigate or prevent climate change. But long-term climate change effects can affect the scope of protection offered to species threatened by climate change or to protections required for waters of the United States affected by climate change.
- The National Environmental Policy Act requires an assessment of the environmental impacts of major actions by the federal government, and this assessment may include a review of potential impacts by or to climate change.
- Tort law actions against emitters of greenhouse gases may not proceed under federal common law because the federal Clean Air Act has displaced those

types of lawsuits. It remains to be seen whether state or local governmental plaintiffs can successfully pursue similar claims under solely state law in state or federal courts.

- Similarly, public trust doctrine lawsuits to force more aggressive actions by the government against climate change are actively underway in federal court, but have not yet yielded a definitive verdict or award.

Chapter 4

Water Pollution

Roadmap

- Understand how the Clean Water Act controls discharges of pollutants into waters of the United States by requiring persons who cause them to obtain permits.
- Grasp how the Clean Water Act requires states to choose the water quality standards for water bodies within their borders, find out whether those water bodies meet the standards, and then compel additional pollution reductions (if needed) to attain the standards.
- Learn how the Clean Water Act protects certain wetlands from dredging or filling activities through a separate permit system implemented by the U.S. Army Corps of Engineers.
- Understand how the Clean Water Act allows the U.S. Environmental Protection Agency to delegate to states the responsibility to issue, oversee, and enforce permits for discharges of pollutants within their borders.
- See how the Clean Water Act requires operators to also obtain permits to control discharges of pollutants contained in storm water that runs off from their facilities.
- Explore how the Clean Water Act requires immediate reports of spills of pollutants to waters of the United States if they exceed a certain amount within 24 hours.
- Learn how the Clean Water Act relies on a combination of self-reporting, governmental enforcement, and citizen suits to assure compliance with the Act's requirements.

The federal Clean Water Act is one of the most ambitious statutes in U.S. environmental law. When Congress passed the progenitor of the Clean Water Act in 1972, it boldly declared that the statute would restore the quality of the nation's waters by eliminating discharges of pollutants into surface waters. Our legislators went even further by setting an ultimate goal of eliminating *all* discharges of pollutants into the nation's navigable waters. While the Clean Water Act has not yet met its original lofty goals, it remains one of the central statutes in U.S. environmental regulation and a keystone to the protection of water resources that fall under federal regulatory jurisdiction.

This chapter reviews the Clean Water Act's most important features for the legal options and strategies pursued by industry, environmental advocates, and governmental agencies to protect water quality. Like many federal environmental statutes, the Clean Water Act actually consists of several subprograms within a larger statutory framework. These subprograms include:

(i) a national pollutant discharge elimination system that requires permits or authorizations for discharges of pollutants from point sources (including indirect sources who discharge to treatment facilities);

(ii) ambient water quality standard programs to assure that rivers, lakes, streams, and coastal waters remain suitable for their designated uses by keeping the pollutants they receive from point and non-point sources to less than a total maximum daily load that they can safely sustain;

(iii) a separate permit program under the U.S. Army Corps of Engineers to protect wetlands that fall under federal jurisdiction; and

(iv) a permit program to control discharges of storm water that may come into contact with potential pollutants at facilities that discharge them through point sources.

Our review also explores how the Clean Water Act stitches these subprograms together through an integrated framework that allows states to assume a primary role in issuing permits and enforcing compliance, authorizes EPA to oversee and enforce those standards if states fall short, and empowers citizens to bring their own lawsuits when facilities or governments fail to satisfy their permit conditions or statutory obligations.

I. The National Pollutant Discharge Elimination System Permit Program

The Clean Water Act builds on a simple, yet sweeping, command: it forbids the discharge of any pollutant from a point source into a navigable water without authorization or a permit. This statutory dictate has led to the creation of a comprehensive permitting system that requires every facility that discharges pollutants into U.S. waters to obtain a National Pollutant Discharge Elimination System (NPDES) permit or its equivalent under a state program. The brevity of the Clean Water Act's no-discharge command, however, hides the complexity of its deceptively simple terms. Each of them—"discharge," "pollutant," "point source," and "navigable water"—is a term of art with an extensive regulatory and caselaw pedigree.

A. The Building Blocks of the No-Discharge Mandate

The Clean Water Act's NPDES permit system relies on jurisdictional gatekeepers that modulate the program's scope and application. Each of those foundational terms requires a deeper examination.

"*Discharge.*" The Clean Water Act specifies that the discharge of a pollutant means "any addition" of a pollutant to navigable waters. 33 U.S.C. § 1362(12). While the courts and EPA have construed "discharge" and "addition" broadly, the terms carry important limits. For example, the core meaning of "addition" means that a discharge must introduce a new material into the water body (or increase the amount or variety of materials already present). This limit implies that a facility that simply draws up pollutants via an intake stream and then discharges them back into the same water body will not trigger an NPDES permit requirement. 40 C.F.R. § 403.15; *Los Angeles Flood Control District v. Natural Resources Defense Council*, 568 U.S. 78 (2013). Based on a similar rationale, water discharges from dams do not "add" pollutants even if they damage the temperature or dissolved oxygen to the receiving water body. *National Wildlife Federation v. Consumers Power Co.*, 862 F.2d 580 (6th Cir. 1988). EPA has also clarified this principle through a regulation that excludes "water transfers"—i.e., conveying or connecting waters of the United States without any intervening commercial or industrial use—from regulation under the Clean Water Act. 40 C.F.R. pt. 122.

"*Pollutant.*" The Clean Water Act continues its broad approach by defining "pollutant" to include a broad swath of materials and contaminants, 33 U.S.C. § 1362(6), and the courts have followed suit. The capacious term now includes everything from heat, acidity, and toxicity to virtually any solid substance (including construction debris and animal carcasses). *Natural Resources Defense Council v. EPA*, 859 F.2d 156 (D.C. Cir. 1988).

"*Point source.*" To focus regulatory attention on discharges from specific facilities (rather than general runoff), the Clean Water Act requires NPDES permits only for discharges from "point sources." The statute broadly defines this term to include "any discernable, confined and discrete conveyance . . . from which pollutants are or may be discharged." 33 U.S.C. § 1362(14). As a result, the NPDES program can apply to almost any natural or man-made conduit through which pollutants may discharge, including ditches, sewers, gullies, channels, pipes, and gutters. Because the statute expressly includes sources where pollutants "may be" discharged, it includes conveyances that only rarely or intermittently discharge pollutants. The term can even extend to mobile sources such as railcars, trucks, and construction vehicles. *United States v. West Indies Transp., Inc.*, 127 F.3d 299 (3d Cir. 1997). It does not include, however, discharges directly from an individual person (at least for criminal liability under the Clean Water Act). *United States v. Plaza Health Laboratories, Inc.*, 3 F.3d 643 (2d Cir. 1993) (Clean Water Act did not require NPDES permit for person who left vials of medical waste on riverbank to be carried away by the tide).

"*Navigable waters.*" This last prerequisite for Clean Water Act jurisdiction has proven, by far, the most problematic. The statute begins by unhelpfully defining "navigable waters" as simply "waters of the United States." 33 U.S.C. § 1362(7). This definition simply restates the test for federal jurisdiction over interstate waters, which has long spurred controversy and litigation. When EPA and the U.S. Army Corps of Engineers attempted to assert jurisdiction over isolated waterbodies solely within state jurisdiction, or over wetlands not immediately adjacent or connected to traditional navigable waters, the U.S. Supreme Court responded with a series of fractured decisions that yielded an unclear test for determining whether some questionable water bodies fell under federal regulation. For example, in *Rapanos v. United States,* 547 U.S. 715 (2006), the Court issued a plurality opinion by Justice Scalia that limited Clean Water Act jurisdiction to traditional water bodies that contain, or directly connect to, flowing waters. The sole concurrence, by Justice Kennedy, instead allowed regulation of water bodies with a "significant nexus" to traditional waters. EPA and the U.S. Army Corps of Engineers responded with an extensive effort to promulgate a Waters of the United States (WOTUS) Rule to clarify their interpretations of the statutory term. 80 Fed. Reg. 37054, 37104-05 (June 29, 2015). The agencies finalized their WOTUS Rule in 2015, but—after several federal court challenges, the issuance of a stay against the WOTUS Rule, and an intervening election—EPA and the Corps have postponed the effective date of the regulation until February 6, 2020. 83 Fed. Reg. 5200 (Feb. 6, 2018). Both agencies have also announced their intent to withdraw and replace the WOTUS Rule in a future rulemaking. 82 Fed. Reg. 34899 (July 27, 2017). Thus, as discussed further below, at this writing the precise parameters of the phrase "navigable waters" remain uncertain as the term is applied to wetland areas.

Notably, "navigable waters" have been held not to include groundwater. As a result, discharges into groundwater do not require NPDES permits. State laws and programs, however, frequently include groundwater within waters of the state protected by permit requirements, and the federal courts have recently emphasized that the Clean Water Act can require NPDES permits (or equivalent state permits) if a discharge to groundwater conveys pollutants to a water of the United States hydraulically connected to the groundwater. *See, e.g., Hawaii Wildlife Fund v. County of Maui,* 886 F.3d 737 (9th Cir. Feb. 1, 2018).

B. NPDES Permits

An NPDES permit essentially gives an operator permission to discharge specific pollutants from particular outfalls into an identified navigable water. While most NPDES permits last for five years, EPA regulations typically extend the operation of an expired NPDES permit while the agency reviews a renewal application or submission for a new permit. This review period can last for years—often exceeding the period of the original NPDES permit itself. However, state agencies issuing their own analogs of NPDES permits under delegated programs may have differing durations and renewal requirements.

To obtain an NPDES permit (or its state equivalent), an operator must first submit a detailed permit application. EPA application forms, for example, seek extensive information about the operator, the facility, the production process that generates the discharge, the likely pollutants that the discharge will contain, how the facility plans to treat the pollutants prior to discharge (if needed), and the nature and quality of the receiving water body. 40 C.F.R. § 122.21. State permit applications under delegated programs must include, at a minimum, the same information. 40 C.F.R. § 123.25(a)(4).

An NPDES permit contains several typical conditions. Most important, the permit will include enforceable limits on the pollutants that it can discharge in its effluent. In addition, the permit will set out reporting requirements for both routine discharges (including discharge monitoring reports, discussed below) and unanticipated spills, and—at some facilities—best management practices that the operator must maintain. Beyond these core requirements, NPDES permits will contain standard provisions that govern routine concerns such as imposing a duty to properly operate and maintain systems, inspection and entry requirements, and defenses for upset and bypass situations that cause discharges that exceed the permit's limits. 40 C.F.R. §§ 122.41–50.

Beyond these standard permit terms, an NPDES permit will set its effluent pollutant limits based on treatment technologies that are feasible and economically achievable for the discharger's industrial sector. These technology-driven limits define the baseline for any discharges from the facility, and the technology selected will vary based on whether the facility is new or existing, and whether the pollutant is conventional (such as grease, pH, or suspended solids) or toxic. 33 U.S.C. § 1311(b)(1)(A), (2)(A), (2)(E); 33 U.S.C. § 1316. In addition to these technology treatment standards, the permit will frequently require the discharge to test the toxicity of the whole effluent through a biological assay test. Under such a whole effluent toxicity test, the discharger will immerse certain sensitive fish or shrimp in the effluent to see whether it harms or kills them. 40 C.F.R. § 122.44(d)(1)(iv).

To assure that the facility's discharge meets applicable requirements, an NPDES permit will also specify the type and frequency of tests that the operator must perform on the facility's effluent. The data resulting from these tests must be reported to EPA or the relevant state agency in a routine Discharge Monitoring Report, or DMR. An operator must submit a DMR even if its data shows a violation of the permit, and intentional false reports or misrepresentations in a DMR can trigger criminal liability under the Clean Water Act.

While NPDES permits provide the central engine for Clean Water Act compliance, they are not the statute's sole tool. The Clean Water Act also allows EPA and states to use alternative means to authorize discharges that do not require the full panoply of NPDES permitting review. For example, EPA has established streamlined and simplified processes to allow operators with routine and non-threatening discharges to obtain authorization by submitting a notice to the agency or meeting generic standard conditions. These tools can include general permits (which are frequently used for storm water discharges, discussed below), permits-by-rule, and standard permits.

C. Permit Shields

One important, and oft-recurring, issue about NPDES permits focuses on how much protection they provide. In particular, if a facility's NPDES permit is silent about a particular pollutant that the operator identified (directly or indirectly) in a permit application, would a discharge containing that unlisted pollutant violate the Clean Water Act's no-discharge prohibition? In short, the federal courts have generally ruled that operators can discharge "pollutants not specifically listed in their permits so long as they comply with the appropriate reporting requirements and abide by any new limitations when imposed on such pollutants." *See, e.g., Atlantic States Legal Foundation, Inc. v. Eastman Kodak Co.*, 12 F.3d 353 (2d Cir.), *cert. denied*, 114 S. Ct. 62 (1994). This permit shield, however, does not extend to operators who fail to strictly comply with their disclosure requirements or don't disclose the pollutant to the regulator in their permit applications. Some permits may also completely prohibit all discharges of any pollutant unless they expressly authorize such pollutant releases.

D. Variances

Given the wide differences in industrial operators and the types of processes they use, it's no surprise that they sometimes cannot meet effluent discharge limits set out by EPA because they don't (or can't) use the pollution control technology selected by the agency. In these circumstances, the Clean Water Act empowers EPA to give variances to operators who face "fundamentally different factors" that would justify a special exemption from technology-based limits (including pretreatment obligations, as discussed below). 33 U.S.C. § 1311(n).

This exemption process, however, has important limitations. For example, EPA cannot allow a variance from limits that assure the receiving water body meets its overall water quality standards. And the variance process requires the applicant to prove that the factors relevant to its facility are fundamentally different from the ones considered in developing the facility's effluent limitations guidelines (e.g., the nature of the pollutants in the discharge, the volume of the discharge, the energy requirements of the treatment technology, the environmental impacts of the control technology, or the age, size, land space, and configuration of the facility). 40 C.F.R. §§ 125.30–32. It is important to note that an operator cannot obtain such a variance simply because the cost of complying would force the facility to shut down. 40 C.F.R. § 125.31. As a result, EPA has infrequently given variances based on an operator's assertion that fundamentally different factors apply to its facility.

E. Indirect Discharges

Not all discharges go directly to water bodies. In fact, some of the largest and most challenging effluent streams go instead to centralized wastewater treatment facilities that have the resources, expertise, and technology needed to properly treat the streams. Most of the largest volume domestic sewage streams from urban areas, for example, go to publicly owned treatment works (POTWs) that treat the wastewater prior to discharging it into rivers or coastal waters. Up to 80 percent of U.S. wastewaters go to POTWs for treatment, and this large share includes significant discharges from industrial users.

The Clean Water Act regulates these indirect discharges under a separate pretreatment program that operates differently from the NPDES program.

Under this pretreatment regime, the POTW enters into a contract with, or issues a permit to, its customer to impose limits on influent streams sent to the POTW. In effect, the POTW directly implements these discharge limits for pretreatment rather than EPA or the relevant state (although these agencies retain ultimate enforcement authority). 33 U.S.C. § 1319; 40 C.F.R. § 403.10(f)(1). The POTW's operator then must obtain an NPDES permit that governs its own effluent discharges resulting from the treatment of its customer's wastewaters. As a result, the POTW may violate its own NPDES permit and incur liability if one of its upstream customers sends it an effluent that disrupts the treatment plant—which gives the POTW a strong incentive to assure that its upstream customers comply with their permits and contracts.

To assure that upstream discharges don't send effluent to POTWs that will disrupt their treatment processes, the Clean Water Act specifically prohibits certain discharges and acts by indirect dischargers. For example, the statute generally prohibits an industrial user from sending any pollutant to a POTW that causes either "pass through" (i.e., conveyance of the pollutant occurs without adequate treatment) or results in an "upset" (i.e., the pollutant disrupts or shuts down the POTW's treatment process). 40 C.F.R. §§ 403.5(a)(1), (k), (p). In addition, EPA's regulations impose eight specific prohibitions that help avoid interference with downstream POTW operations, including discharges that create fire or explosion hazards or damage structures at the POTW via corrosion. 40 C.F.R. § 403.5(b).

II. Ambient Water Quality Standards and the Total Maximum Daily Load Process

In addition to technology-based limitations and NPDES permits for specific discharges, the Clean Water Act also establishes a fail-safe to assure that discharges—even if properly permitted—do not overload a water body that receives multiple outfalls. Essentially, the statute requires states to decide the proper use for each water body within its borders. These uses can include common activities such as fishing, recreation, drinking water supplies, industrial, agricultural, or other uses. 33 U.S.C. § 1313(c)(2); 40 C.F.R. § 131.10(a). After setting the water body's uses, the state then identifies the physical, chemical, and biological parameters of the water necessary for it to support those uses. For example, the state may set a water quality standard concentration limit for a particular pollutant that, once exceeded, would render the water unfit for recreation or fishing. These state criteria typically rely on underlying federal water quality criteria that establish limits for more than 150 pollutants. 33 U.S.C. § 1314(a)(1).

Armed with these water quality standards, EPA or the state then back-calculates how much of a particular pollutant that water body can receive without exceeding the standard—its total maximum daily load (TMDL) of that pollutant. If the water body already fails to meet its water quality standard, the permitting agency then essentially sets (or revises) permit limits for future or ongoing discharges to assure that the water body attains its designated use. 33 U.S.C. § 1313(d). The Clean Water Act requires states or EPA to identify which water bodies are impaired, identify TMDLs for those impaired water bodies, submit the list to EPA for approval, and then assure that permits for discharges to the impaired water body remain collectively under their TMDLs.

The TMDL program has proven enormously controversial. States have generally lagged in identifying impaired water bodies and preparing TMDLs for each of them. This inaction has triggered dozens of lawsuits to force states to move, and EPA's efforts to streamline and implement the program through regulatory revisions have triggered its own firestorm of lawsuits and opposition. Despite efforts by EPA to modernize the program and promote cooperative planning and implementation with states, proposed regulatory revisions have collapsed under litigation challenges (including a final rule to revise its TMDL regulations in 2000 that the agency subsequently withdrew). *Withdrawal of Water Quality Planning and Management Regulation*, 68 Fed. Reg. 13608 (March 19, 2003). As a result, EPA has used essentially the same regulatory framework for implementing TMDLs since 1992—more than a quarter-century ago.

III. Wetlands Permitting

The Clean Water Act's prohibition on unpermitted discharges also bars the placement of dredge or fill material into certain wetlands that fall within the definition of "navigable waters" as part of the waters of the United States. As noted previously, the scope of waters included in this term is hotly contested, and the requirement for a permit to discharge dredge or fill materials into wetlands—which, by definition, may not consist solely of flowing waters—sparks some of the greatest controversy under the Clean Water Act. Some aspects of the definition of "wetland," such as the requirements that they have hydrophytic vegetation, hydric soil, and periodic inundations with water, do not raise serious objections. The core jurisdiction concept—that the wetland has some connection or proximity to waters of the United States that fall under federal jurisdiction—is far murkier and disputed. EPA passed its Clean Water Rule in 2015 to clarify the definition of "wetlands," but EPA and the U.S. Army Corps of Engineers have proposed to withdraw that rule-making (as noted above).

If a wetland falls under the jurisdiction of the Clean Water Act, no one can discharge fill or dredge material into the wetland without a permit issued by the U.S. Army Corps of Engineers under section 404 of the Clean Water Act. 33 U.S.C. § 1344. These permits cover only the actual discharge or placement of dredged or fill materials, and as a result they are not required for incidental fallback of dredged materials during wetland dredging operations. Notably, the incidental fallback concept does not exclude from regulation the redeposit of dredged materials into a wetland or other water body, and EPA and the Corps have established a regulatory presumption that any mechanized ditching, channelization, or excavation with discharges greater than incidental fallback will need a Section 404 permit. 33 C.F.R. § 323.2(d)(2)(i); 40 C.F.R. § 232.2(2)(i).

Permits for dredge and fill activities can follow two paths. First, the Corps has established nationwide and general permits for categories of discharges that occur routinely and do not typically significantly injure the environment. These nationwide permits can authorize the construction of minor roads, oil and gas structures, backfilling of utility lines, and certain hydropower projects. To qualify for a nationwide permit, the operator typically must provide notice to the Corps or, for some permits, simply comply with the general conditions of a self-executing nationwide permit.

The second path, for dredge and fill operations that do not qualify for nationwide or general permits, requires the operator to obtain an individual permit for its specific discharge. The standards for an individual permit can be very demanding. For example, the Corps will typically assess a permit application to evaluate its probable impacts on the public interest and the environment (including balancing of "conservation, economics, aesthetics, general environmental concerns, wetlands,") and numerous other values. The Corps cannot reject a permit solely based on its economic effects unrelated to environmental impacts. It will only authorize the discharge (per EPA guidelines) if the applicant proves that there is no "practical alternative to the proposed discharge which would have less adverse impact on the aquatic system." 40 C.F.R. § 230.10(a). EPA has the authority to veto a proposed permit under Section 404(c) of the Clean Water Act. 33 U.S.C. § 1344(c).

Once an applicant has taken all practicable steps to minimize the harm caused by the proposed filling or dredging, it must then mitigate any remaining damage. Pursuant to the no-net-loss policy followed by EPA and the Corps, the Corps must determine whether the applicant has avoided potential impacts to the maximum extent practicable. After that, the remaining unavoidable impacts must have been mitigated "to the extent appropriate and practicable," which can obligate the applicant to compensate financially for lost environmental values in the wetlands and/or offset the harms through wetlands restoration or creation through compensatory mitigation. U.S. Army Corps of Engineers and U.S. Environmental Protection Agency, *Compensatory Mitigation for Losses of Aquatic Resources*, 73 Fed. Reg. 19594 (April 10, 2008).

IV. Storm Water Discharges

Discharges of storm water—capricious, voluminous, hard to control—have posed special challenges for the Clean Water Act. Congress has set out separate requirements to handle them. As you will remember, the Clean Water Act requires permits only for discharges of pollutants to navigable waters through point sources. If a rainfall generates storm water that does not contain a pollutant, or that does not discharge from a point source such as a ditch, gulley, or culvert, the statute does not require the facility operator to obtain a permit. However, if rainfall comes into contact with open industrial operations or contaminants, and discharges through a point source, the facility operator will typically need to obtain a storm water permit.

Given that virtually every industrial facility will likely have some storm water that arguably could trigger jurisdiction under the Clean Water Act, the statute and regulations set out two pathways to authorize discharges. First, a discharger can apply for coverage under a general permit designed to cover broad swaths of industrial sectors with minimal individual information or paperwork requirements. For example, EPA has issued a multisector general storm-water permit that covers 29 industrial sectors. Other baseline general permits protect other industrial categories and operations. These permits generally impose less stringent requirements and less burdensome disclosure requirements than tailored individual permits.

Second, a facility that does not qualify for the general permit can seek an individual storm water permit. These permits may require detailed disclosures about the facility, data collection and analysis of its discharges, and sampling during storm events. As a result, preparation of an individual storm water permit application can prove costly, burdensome, and slow. 40 C.F.R. § 122.26(c).

V. Spill Reporting and Responses

As part of its overall purpose to prevent discharges of pollutants into waters of the United States, the Clean Water Act sets out separate requirements that focus specifically on accidental or unanticipated spills and releases. In particular, the Act tackles the problem of accidental pollution with three tools: mandated prevention and contingency planning to keep spills from happening in the first place, reporting obligations to alert the appropriate authorities and assure a speedy response, and liability for spills to assure that responsible parties undertake remediation and shoulder the costs of response.

Any facility that manages or stores more than 13,200 gallons of oil above ground, or 42,000 gallons underground, is required by the Clean Water Act to prepare a Spill Prevention Control and Countermeasure (SPCC) Plan so long as the facility can reasonably be expected to discharge oil in harmful quantities into or upon navigable waters because of its location. 33 U.S.C. § 1321(b)(1); 40 C.F.R. § 112.1(b)–(d)(1). A SPCC Plan typically identifies the employees responsible for spill prevention who will report to facility management, recount recent prior spills, and specify the types of spill control strategies and containment structures that will contain any releases. Facility operators must prepare, submit to EPA, and implement a SPCC Plan within six months after beginning operations. They must also update the plan when the facility's design, operation, or maintenance changes in a way that materially affects the facility's potential to discharge oil. 40 C.F.R. §§ 112.3(b), 112.5.

When a spill occurs, the Clean Water Act requires a person in charge of the facility to report a release to navigable waters or adjoining shorelines of a pollutant that exceeds a reportable quantity. EPA has designated reportable quantities for more than 300 substances, and both EPA and the Corps have defined a reportable quantity of oil as any amount that causes a film or sheen on the receiving waters or that violates an applicable water quality standard. 40 C.F.R. § 110.3. While the person in charge must use a rolling 24-hour period to determine whether the spill exceeds a reportable quantity, once the spill crosses that threshold it must be reported immediately. Failure to report such a spill is a criminal act potentially punishable by up to five years in prison. 33 U.S.C. § 1321(b)(5).

Finally, if a spill occurs, the owners or operators of a facility that releases the oil into waters of the United States or adjoining shorelines face strict liability for penalties, the costs of responding to the spill, and any natural resources damages caused by the spill. Civil judicial penalties can reach up to either $46,192 per day per violation, or up to $1,848 per barrel of discharged oil. If the spill resulted from gross negligence or willful misconduct, the penalties escalate to $184,767 per day per violation and $5,543 per barrel of oil. 33 U.S.C. §§ 1321(b)(7); 40 C.F.R. § 19.4. However, facility owners or operators can avail themselves of some limited statutory defenses to liability such as act of God, act of war, negligence on the part of the United States, or an act or omission of a third party. 33 U.S.C. § 1321(f)(2).

VI. Delegation, Enforcement, and Citizen Suits

The Clean Water Act, like other federal environmental statutes, allows states to take a lead role in implementing and enforcing its requirements. If a state wishes to apply for delegation to take primacy for NPDES permits issued within its borders, it must first submit a demonstration to EPA that its laws, program, agency, resources, and enforcement authorities roughly equate to EPA's authorities. In particular, the state must show that it has a viable and functioning civil and criminal enforcement program and a well-developed administrative enforcement system. 33 U.S.C. § 1321(b)(7); 40 C.F.R. § 123.27(a). While the state's environmental program does not have to duplicate EPA's regulatory requirements, it must meet minimum requirements imposed by the federal program. States can, however, impose more stringent or broader requirements beyond EPA's standards.

Given the overlapping enforcement and jurisdictional authorities between federal and state agencies when EPA has delegated primacy for a water permitting program to the state, enforcement can prove complicated. In states with delegated programs, EPA retains the right to initiate enforcement even if the state has chosen not to enforce. To do so, EPA must first give prior notice to the state and then allow the state 30 days to bring its own enforcement action. Once these conditions are met, EPA can initiate its own "overfiling" on state enforcement action (or inaction). The state and EPA can each bring their own parallel enforcement actions, but EPA generally cannot bring a duplicate enforcement action once the state has obtained a final judgment to resolve the action. If a state routinely and consistently fails to enforce against permit violations, EPA can take over enforcement within the state until the state agency begins to adequately enforce its permit program again. EPA can also seek to revoke the state's delegation of enforcement authority in egregious cases.

Beyond the conventional enforcement tools of civil, criminal, and administrative actions, the Clean Water Act authorizes citizens to bring their own enforcement actions as "private attorneys general." Under Section 505 of the statute, any person with "an interest which is or may be adversely affected" can sue any other person for violation of an effluent standard, limit, or order (including permit discharge limits). 33 U.S.C. § 1365. The statute also empowers citizens to sue EPA if it fails to perform a nondiscretionary duty.

Given the limited resources available to state environmental programs and the potential for political controversy, the engine of citizen suits has allowed numerous enforcement actions that might otherwise not have gotten to court. If a citizen or environmental group can meet federal standing requirements (typically by showing an ongoing violation that directly affects its personal, physical, economic, or aesthetic interests), it can often sue a facility operator for exceeding permit limits by using the facility's own discharge monitoring reports to the state or EPA as evidence of a violation. To initiate a citizen suit, however, the citizen must give the alleged violator and the state agency or EPA prior notice of the lawsuit, and the state is authorized take over the lawsuit by initiating its own diligent prosecution of the violation. 33 U.S.C. § 1365(b).

Checkpoints

- The Clean Water Act prohibits any discharge of a pollutant to navigable waters through a point source.
  - Any owner or operator of a facility that wants to discharge wastewaters into a water body under federal jurisdiction must first obtain an NPDES permit from EPA or a state agency in delegated states.
  - All of these terms—"discharge," "pollutant," "point source," and "navigable waters"—have specific regulatory definitions that mirror the broad statutory definition for each term, but that incorporate important exceptions.
    - NPDES permits are not required for discharges that simply move water within a water body without adding pollutants, or that go to isolated water bodies that do not constitute "navigable waters."
    - NPDES permits also are not needed for discharges vented solely to groundwater unconnected with navigable waters.
  - NPDES permits establish specific limits for pollutants in the discharge based on both technology standards set by EPA and on whether the receiving water is clean enough for its selected use, as reflected in state water quality standards and total maximum daily loads.
  - NPDES permits typically last for five years, and they must be renewed if the discharge continues past that time.
- If a facility does not discharge its effluent directly into navigable waters and instead sends it off-site to a centralized wastewater treatment plant or publicly owned treatment works (POTW), it must first satisfy pretreatment standards.
  - The POTW operator will give the facility operator a permit or contract that spells out the specific contaminants (and concentrations of them) that the facility's effluent can contain.
  - In addition, the effluent cannot disrupt the POTW's operations by creating either a bypass (where the pollutants pass through untreated) or upset (where the pollutants impair or shut down the POTW's treatment process).
  - The POTW operator discharges under its own NPDES permit for its treatment process. If a facility's effluent causes the POTW operator to violate its permit, the POTW may either bring an enforcement action or initiate a breach of contract lawsuit against the facility if its discharges violated the POTW's pretreatment agreement or order.
- In addition to setting discharge limits on a site-by-site basis, the state must also identify whether the receiving water body is already impaired by other discharges and pollution.
  - If that water body is impaired because its current pollution levels make it unfit for its designated use, the state must determine how much pollution that water body can safely absorb on a daily basis. The state then uses this

number to set the Total Maximum Daily Load (TMDL) limit for the water body.

  - EPA or the state will then back-calculate how much additional pollution a discharging facility will need to remove from an effluent stream to bring the water body into compliance with the applicable water quality standard. This can require additional reductions beyond the existing NPDES permit's treatment requirements.

- The Clean Water Act also restricts the placement of dredge and fill materials into wetlands under federal jurisdiction.
  - These permits, authorized under Section 404 of the Clean Water Act, are issued by the U.S. Army Corps of Engineers. But EPA retains authority to veto proposed Section 404 permits that do not meet environmental standards.
  - Determining whether a wetland falls within "navigable waters" regulated under the Clean Water Act is often a difficult task, and it has generated heated and lengthy controversy in rulemaking proceedings as well as frequent litigation.
- Owners or operators of facilities or vessels must report a spill or release of a pollutant or oil to navigable waters under the Clean Water Act. Spills become reportable if they exceed a reportable quantity within a 24-hour period (although an operator must report a spill immediately once it exceeds the regulatory threshold). EPA has set reportable quantities for more than 300 chemicals by regulation; and (as noted above) a spill of oil to waters must be reported if it creates a sheen or slick on the water.
- In addition to enforcement actions by the state agency, operators who violate their NPDES permits may face administrative actions or lawsuits from EPA or citizen suits. The Clean Water Act authorizes citizens to sue permit holders for violating their permit's terms. Citizens may also sue EPA for failure to perform a nondiscretionary duty under the statute.

Chapter 5

The Comprehensive Environmental Response, Compensation, and Liability Act (CERCLA)

Roadmap

- Understand the response action process implemented by EPA to respond to hazardous substance contamination.
- Learn who are "potentially responsible parties" (PRPs) that may be liable for the cleanup of facilities contaminated by hazardous substances.
- Comprehend what expenses PRPs may be responsible for.
- Understand how Congress and the federal courts have treated CERCLA liability in cases involving multiple responsible parties.
- Grasp how the tort law concept of contribution has been incorporated in CERCLA cases.
- Learn the substantive and procedural aspects of the statute that guide settlement of CERCLA claims.

I. Introduction

In the late 1970s, a series of highly publicized environmental disasters jarringly introduced the American public to the dangers created by the haphazard disposal of hazardous chemical waste. It quickly became evident that haphazard dumping of hazardous materials into unprotected ditches, pits, ponds, lagoons, landfills, and other places posed a serious threat to drinking water supplies, property, natural resources, and human health. The public reacted to this newly realized peril with anguish and anger. The perceived "hazardous waste crisis" that began in 1978 at Love Canal in New York State created a political uproar that pressured elected and appointed public officials to respond promptly and effectively to the risks created at abandoned hazardous waste sites. The public further demanded that the individuals or entities responsible for hazardous waste release be held to account.

Following a vigorous 18-month litigation effort by EPA and the U.S. Department of Justice to use the imminent hazard provision of the Resource Conservation and Recovery Act as a legal tool to compel hazardous waste site cleanups, and lengthy congressional debates and negotiations among lawmakers, Congress passed the Comprehensive Environmental Response, Compensation and Liability Act ("CERCLA" or the "Superfund Act") in December 1980. This statute was amended several times thereafter—most notably in the Superfund Amendments and Reauthorization Act of 1986—to correct problems with EPA's implementation of the law and clarify ambiguous provisions of the initial statute.

This chapter describes the most important provisions of CERCLA and the government-managed program that implements it. After considering the legal measures established by the statute for responding to hazardous waste spills and hazardous conditions at abandoned dumpsites, it focuses on various aspects of CERCLA's liability scheme. Those include the overall structure and common elements of Superfund liability, the identity of responsible parties and what they are liable for, the liabilities of multiple responsible parties, contribution and private cost recovery lawsuits, and the settlement of CERCLA enforcement actions against responsible parties.

II. The Response Action Process

A crucial feature of CERCLA is the authority it gives to federal authorities to investigate and evaluate facilities at which hazardous substances are located, and to take direct actions to remedy releases of substances that will endanger health or the environment. The statute directed the president (and, by delegation, EPA) to prepare a plan to establish a "national oil and hazardous substances contingency plan" (commonly referred to as the "National Contingency Plan" or the NCP) to guide the implementation of those legal tools. CERCLA § 105, 42 U.S.C. § 9605. EPA complied with Congress's directive by comprehensively revising and extending a preexisting plan for responding to oil spills into the nation's waters. The NCP that resulted provides detailed guidelines for the investigation, evaluation, and cleanup process that are at the heart of CERCLA. *See* 40 C.F.R. pt. 300.

Under the Plan, Superfund response actions begin with the discovery of a release (or threatened release) of hazardous substances at a specific geographic location. Unless there is an emergency at the site, EPA will evaluate the dangers that it poses to determine whether a short-term "removal action" is needed to protect public health and the environment. Such an action often involves placing a fence around a site, removing and safely disposing of leaking drums of hazardous materials, and/or other measures that can be taken relatively promptly.

Where EPA concludes that a further, long-term response is needed at a facility, the Agency will begin what is known as a "remedial action." The process of remedial action, which can proceed in parallel with or following a removal action, begins with a Preliminary Assessment/Site Investigation (or "PA/SI") where data is gathered to assess the severity of the risks posed by the site. Using those data, EPA employs a so-called "hazard ranking system" as a screening device to assess "the potential for releases of uncontrolled hazardous substances to cause human health or environmental damage . . ." Hazardous substance releases that exceed a given threshold score are eligible to be placed on a National Priorities List ("the NPL") and become a candidate for remedial action funded by the Superfund. *See* 40 C.F.R. pt. 300, Appendix B.

Following the NPL listing of a facility, EPA proceeds to prepare a remedial investigation/feasibility study (an "RI/FS") to assess in greater detail the environmental and health risks posed at the site, and to develop and evaluate potential remedial actions. The Agency then proceeds to select one or more specific long-term remedial measures, applying a set of criteria set forth in the NCP. *See* CERCLA § 121, 42 U.S.C. § 9621 and 40 C.F.R. § 300.430(e)(9)(3). Following public comment, the remedial action the Agency has selected is memorialized in a Record of Decision ("ROD"), and EPA designs and implements its chosen remedy in a Remedial Design/Remedial Action ("RD/RA"). Once all response actions have been carried out, EPA may delete a presumably "clean" site from the NPL. However, at some "de-listed" sites, periods of operation and maintenance activities are still required; and where hazardous substances are left in place at a site, the statute requires the agency to review the completed remedial action every five years to ascertain whether the remedy continues to protect human health and the environment. *See* 42 U.S.C. § 9621(c).

A. Remedies

When the Superfund Act was amended in 1984 by the Superfund Amendments and Reauthorization Act ("SARA"), Congress established the degree of cleanup that must be the result of remedial actions. A product of congressional dissatisfaction with some of EPA's initial remedial decisions, SARA requires that most cleanups comply with "applicable or relevant and appropriate requirements" established in other federal and state environmental laws. *See* 40 U.S.C. § 9621(d), CERCLA § 121(d). Those borrowed cleanup standards are generally referred to by the acronym "ARARs." Where no ARARs exist for a particular hazardous substance released at a Superfund site, EPA generally attempts to protect human health and the environment by setting site-specific remedial goals that eliminate exposures that would produce adverse human health effects.

B. Administrative Response Action Orders

Recognizing the benefits of harnessing private resources to remediate ongoing or threatened hazardous substance releases, Congress provided EPA with potent tools to compel private parties to remedy harmful conditions they created. In situations where the Agency determines that "an actual or threatened release of a hazardous substance from a facility" may be creating "an imminent and substantial endangerment to public health or welfare or the environment," EPA is authorized to require the U.S. Department of Justice to file a civil action in federal court seeking equitable relief. *See* CERCLA § 106(a), 42 U.S.C. § 9606(a). EPA may also issue administrative response action orders to protect public health, welfare, and the environment.

Since the late 1980s, EPA has pursued an "enforcement first policy" in CERCLA matters, relying extensively on administrative orders to secure prompt cleanup actions by responsible parties. Although EPA has a clear preference for reaching negotiated agreements with those parties, it relies on unilateral administrative orders where negotiations fail. Litigation is only rarely initiated to encourage response actions by potentially responsible parties ("PRPs").

Violations of EPA administrative orders can result in severe penalties. The statute provides that a person who willfully violates or refuses to comply with such an order may be liable for civil penalties of up to $25,000 per day—a penalty amount that was increased to $53,907 per day to account for inflation, in accordance with the Federal Civil Penalties Adjustment Act. *See* CERCLA § 106(b)(1), 42 U.S.C. 106(b); 42 U.S.C § 9606(b)(1), and 28 U.S.C. § 2691. Moreover, liable parties that "without sufficient cause" fail to comply with orders that compel them to undertake removal or remedial actions may be liable for punitive damages of up to three times the cleanup costs incurred by the government as a result of their noncompliance. *See* CERCLA § 107(c)(3), 42 U.S.C. § 9607(c)(3). Though these provisions of the statute have been challenged as inconsistent with the due process clause of the Fifth

Amendment, their constitutionality has been upheld by the courts. *See, e.g., General Electric Co. v. Jackson*, 610 F.3d 110 (D.C. Cir. 2010) (recipients of unilateral administrative orders under CERCLA are not entitled to immediately challenge the constitutionality or substance of those orders).

On the other hand, where a respondent complies with an administrative order, but nonetheless believes the order was unlawful, the respondent may petition EPA for reimbursement of its costs of compliance under Superfund. CERCLA § 106(b)(2), 42 U.S.C. § 9606(b)(2). Petitioners who are dissatisfied with EPA's decision may obtain judicial review in a U.S. District Court. Those parties will prevail if they prove that EPA's decision in selecting the response action in question was "arbitrary and capricious" or otherwise not in accordance with law. Alternately, they may receive reimbursement if they can demonstrate that they were not responsible parties as defined by the statute, CERCLA § 106(b)(2)(D), 42 U.S.C. § 9606 (b)(2)(D).

III. CERCLA Liability

A. The Structure and Common Elements of Liability

At section 107(a), 42 U.S.C. § 9607(a), CERCLA makes four categories of parties liable to reimburse response costs incurred by the government. Those are:

(i) the present owner or operator of a facility,
(ii) a past owner or operator of a facility who owned or operated that facility during a period when hazardous substances were disposed there,
(iii) a person who "arranged for disposal or treatment" of their own hazardous substances by another party or entity, and
(iv) a person who accepts or accepted hazardous substances for transport to disposal or treatment facilities or incineration sites from which there is a hazardous substance release that causes the incurrence of response costs.

The term "person" is broadly defined. It includes "an individual, firm, corporation, association, partnership, consortium, joint venture, commercial entity, United States Government, State, municipality, political subdivision of a state, or any interstate body." CERCLA § 101(21), 42 U.S.C. § 9201(21). However, the U.S. Supreme Court has held that States are entitled to immunity from suit, under the Eleventh Amendment, unless they have consented to be sued. *Seminole Tribe of Florida v. Florida,* 517 U.S. 44 (1996).

Under CERCLA, responsible parties are liable where there has been a release or threatened release of a hazardous substance from a facility that has caused the incurrence of response costs. The terms "hazardous substance," "facility," "environment," and "release" are all very broadly defined in the statute. *See* CERCLA §§ 101(8)(9) and (22), 42 U.S.C §§ 9601(8)(9) and (22). Moreover, with regard to "arranger" (or "generator") defendants, the statute is satisfied by proof that hazardous substances "like" those contained in the defendant's waste are found at the site. Proof that the specific substance generated by the defendant was present at the site at the time of disposal is not required. *United States v. Monsanto Co.,* 858 F.2d 160 (4th Cir. 1986). CERCLA applies retroactively to pre-enactment conduct that caused a hazardous substance release, even where that conduct was legal at the time it was undertaken. *See ASARCO LLC v. Goodwin,* 756 F.3d 191 (2d Cir. 2014); *United States v. Dico, Inc.,* 266 F.3d 846 (8th Cir. 2001); and *O'Neil v. Picillo,* 883 F.2d 176 (1st Cir. 1989).

Affirmative defenses to CERCLA liability are extremely limited. PRPs may escape liability only where they can establish that the release or threat of a release in question was caused by "an act of God, an act of war, and act or omission of a third party, or any combination thereof." CERCLA §§ 107(a) and (b), 42 U.S.C. §§ 9607(a) and (b). The statute also constrains the "act of a third party" defense by providing that the third party in question must not be an employee, agent, or contractor of the defendant; and the defendant exercised due care with respect to the hazardous substances, and "took precautions against foreseeable acts or omissions of any such third party and the consequences that could foreseeably result from such acts or omissions." CERCLA § 107(b), 42 U.S.C. § 9607(b).

B. Responsible Parties

1. Owners or Operators

CERCLA defines an "owner or operator" of a facility containing hazardous substances very simply as "any person owning or operating a facility." CERCLA § 101(20)(A), 42 U.S.C. § 9601(20)(A). In addition to title holders of record, the term has been held to include some tenants with sufficient authority over the property in question. *See Commander Oil Corp. v. Barlo Equipment Corp.,* 215 F.3d 31 (2d Cir. 2000). An owning stockholder, who manages a corporation holding legal title to contaminated real property, has been deemed an "owner or operator" for CERCLA purposes. *See New York v. Shore Realty Corp.*, 759 F.2d 1032 (2d Cir. 1985).

However, CERCLA also excludes from liability "a person who, without participating in the management of a facility who holds indicia of ownership primarily to protect his security interest in the facility." CERCLA § 101(20)(A), 42 U.S.C. § 9601(20)(A). The statute defines "participation in management" narrowly, assuring that most common lender activities will not subject lenders to CERCLA liability. It also excludes from the definition of "owner or operator" lenders who take title by foreclosure. CERCLA §§ 101(20)(E) and (F), 42 U.S.C.§§ 9602(20)(E) and (F). The Act further excludes a government agency that "involuntarily acquires title by virtue of its function as a sovereign," such as by escheat or eminent domain, or as a result of tax delinquency. CERCLA § 101(20)(D), 42 U.S.C. § 9601(20)(D).

CERCLA provides limited relief to so-called "innocent landowners," i.e., parties who unwittingly purchased contaminated property. Such owners may escape liability if, at the time they acquired the facility, they did not know and had no reason to know that any hazardous substance had been disposed of "on, in, or at the facility." CERCLA § 101(35)(A), 42 U.S.C. § 9601(35)(A). To establish that the defendant had "no reason to know" of the contamination in question, the defendant must have undertaken, at the time of acquisition, "all appropriate inquiry into the previous ownership and uses of the property consistent with good commercial or customary practice. . . ." *Id.* Moreover, to benefit from the innocent landowner defense, an owner must show that he, she, or it exercised due care and took prudent precautions against the foreseeable acts of third parties.

Another defense from CERCLA liability was created in a set of 2002 amendments to the statute known as the Small Business Liability Relief and Revitalization Act or the Brownfield Amendments of 2002, Pub. L. No. 107-118, 115 Stat. 2356. A major purpose of this legislation was to encourage the redevelopment of "brownfields," i.e., abandoned real property, typically located in urban areas with high unemployment, whose reuse might be complicated by the presence (or potential presence) of a hazardous substance.

Under these 2002 amendments, "bona fide prospective purchasers" are permitted to acquire contaminated brownfield property for redevelopment without incurring CERCLA liability, as long as they satisfy certain conditions. Specifically, they must perform "all appropriate inquiries" prior to purchasing a brownfield site. They must demonstrate that they have no affiliation with a PRP at the site. And they are obligated to comply with applicable land use restrictions, take "reasonable steps" with regard to hazardous substances that affect the property in question, provide all legally required notices, and comply with information requests and administrative subpoenas.

2. *Owners or Operators at the Time of Disposal*

CERCLA includes as responsible parties persons who owned or operated a hazardous substance facility in the past, provided that hazardous substances were disposed of at that facility during the time that they owned or operated it. CERCLA § 107(a)(2), 42 U.S.C. § 9607(a)(2). A party that owned or operated a facility before hazardous substances were deposited there would not be liable.

The term "disposal" is expansively defined in the Act as "the discharge, deposit, injection, dumping, spilling, leaking or placing of any solid or hazardous material into or on any land or water so that such solid waste or hazardous waste or any constituent thereof may enter the environment or be emitted into the air or discharged into any waters, including ground waters." CERCLA § 109(29), 42 U.S.C. § 9601(29) (incorporating by reference the definition of disposal from the Resource Conservation and Recovery Act (RCRA)). Any repositioning or other movement of hazardous substances at a facility has been held to constitute disposal. *See, e.g., Tanglewood East Homeowners v. Charles Thomas, Inc.*, 849 F.2d 1568 (5th Cir. 1988); and *United States v. CDMG Realty Co.*, 96 F.3d 706 (3d Cir. 1996). The federal courts have differed, however, with regard to whether a disposal has taken place where previously deposited hazardous substances migrate through environmental media by "leaking" or "spilling" without affirmative human involvement. *Cf. ABB Industrial Systs., Inc. v. Prime Technology, Inc.*, 120 F.3d 351 (2d Cir. 1997) with *Nurad, Inc. v. William E. Hooper and Sons Co.*, 966 F.2d 837 (4th Cir. 1992).

Parent corporations may be held liable as "operators" under CERCLA where they directly operated a facility in lieu of, or in addition to, their subsidiaries. However, to incur liability the parent corporation must "manage, direct, or conduct operations specifically related to a [subsidiary's] facility." *United States v. Bestfoods*, 524 U.S. 51 (1998).

3. *Arrangers*

CERCLA distinguishes arrangers from both owners or operators and transporters. Arrangers may only be liable where they arrange for disposal or treatment of hazardous substances at facilities owned or operated by *another* party. They can also "arrange" for disposal with a transporter, rather than directly with the owner or operator of a treatment, storage, and disposal facility. CERCLA § 107(a)(3), 42 U.S.C. § 9607(a)(3).

Arranger liability will clearly attach if an entity enters into a transaction for the sole purpose of discarding a hazardous substance that is no longer useful. In contrast, an entity will not be liable as an arranger where it sells a new and useful product to a third party where that third party disposes of the product in a way that causes contamination. *Burlington Northern and Santa Fe Railway Co. v. United States*, 556 U.S. 599 (2009). And a *bona fide* sale of a useful product does not necessarily create arranger liability even if the seller knew that the transaction would result in the disposal of hazardous substances. *Id.; Ekotek Site PRP Comm. v. Self*, 932 F. Supp. 1328 (D. Utah 1996).

In situations where a seller of a hazardous product has some knowledge of its buyer's planned disposal, or where its motives for the sale of a hazardous substance is not clear, courts will conduct a "fact-intensive inquiry" to determine whether the seller falls into the arranger category. *See United States v. Aceto Agricultural Chem. Corp.*, 872 F.3d 1373 (8th Cir. 1989). That inquiry will focus on the extent to which the hazardous product seller entered into the sale of its product with the intention that at least a portion of the product would be "disposed" of within the meaning of the statute. *Burlington Northern and Santa Fe Railway Co. v. United States, supra.*

To be liable as a CERCLA arranger, a person need not arrange for its hazardous substances to be disposed of at the specific facility from which those substances are released. *Ekotek Site PRP Comm. v. Self*, 932 F. Supp. 1328 (D. Utah 1996). Moreover, the hazardous substances in question need not be hazardous waste. *B.F. Goodrich v. Murtha*, 958 F.2d 1192 (2d Cir. 1992). To be a CERCLA arranger, an entity does not necessarily need to actually generate the hazardous substance that was disposed of, *see, e.g., United States v. Bliss*, 667 F. Supp. 1298 (E.D. Mo. 1987), and arranger liability may attach to individual corporate officers or employees who personally make arrangements to dispose of their corporate employer's hazardous substances. *United States v. Northeastern Pharm. and Chem. Co.*, 810 F.2d 726 (8th Cir. 1986).

4. Transporters

Under CERCLA, parties that transport hazardous substances are only liable for releases of those substances from facilities that they themselves have selected. The word "transport" is broadly defined in the statute as "the movement of a hazardous substance by any mode." CERCLA § 101(26), 42 U.S.C. § 9601(26). A person is liable as a transporter not only if it ultimately selects a disposal facility, but also when that party "actively participates in the disposal decision to the extent of having had substantial input into which [disposal] facility was ultimately chosen." *Tippins, Inc. v. USX Corp.*, 37 F.3d 87 (3d Cir. 1994).

C. What Potentially Responsible Parties May Be Responsible For

1. *Government Response Costs*

CERCLA imposes liability on potentially responsible parties (PRPs) for "all costs of removal or remedial action incurred by the United States Government or a State or an Indian tribe not consistent with the National Contingency Plan" ("NCP"). CERCLA § 107(a)(4)(A), 42 U.S.C. § 9607(a)(4)(A). The statute clarifies the meaning of "costs of removal or remedial action" by specifying that reimbursable governmental response costs include costs to government entities associated with: (i) investigations, monitoring, and testing to identify the dangers posed at a facility and the extent of release or threatened release of hazardous substances; (ii) planning and implementation of a response action; and (iii) enforcement of the provisions of CERCLA, including the costs incurred for the staffs of EPA and the Department of Justice. *Id.*

Consistency with the NCP has been held to be the sole criterion for recovery of response costs under CERCLA. *United States v. American Cyanamid Co.*, 786 F. Supp. 152 (D.R.I. 1992). Once the government has presented a *prima facie* case for response costs, the burden shifts to the defendants to identify a particular provision in the NCP with which a particular response action is inconsistent. Even if such an inconsistency can be demonstrated, however, defendants must still show that the cleanup, because of some variance from the NCP, resulted in such "demonstrable excessive costs" that the government's actions were "arbitrary and capricious"; and where the government has actually acted in accordance with the NCP, PRPs may not raise the defense that the government's costs are unreasonable. *Id.*

In addition to the direct costs of investigating threatening conditions at facilities, and planning and implementing hazardous substance cleanups, EPA and other government entities are also entitled to recover their "indirect costs," i.e., costs that are not incurred specifically for a particular response action but that support the administration of the entire Superfund program. At EPA, cost-accountants have created a formula for distributing a portion of these "overhead" costs—e.g., the cost of writing EPA CERCLA guidance documents—to individual response actions.

2. *Response Costs of Nongovernmental Actors*

Responsible parties are liable under CERCLA for "any other necessary costs of response incurred by any other person consistent with the National Contingency Plan." CERCLA § 107(a)(4)(B), 42 U.S.C. § 9607(a)(4)(B). The phrase "other person" (who incurs responsive costs) is obviously a broad term. It includes PRPs who have not been subject to governmental enforcement actions, volunteers who clean up hazardous substances releases even though they would not be liable for failing to do so, and "innocent landowners" who clean up hazardous substances released onto their property by another party or parties.

In contrast to governmental parties, private plaintiffs must affirmatively prove that all cleanup costs they incurred were consistent with the NCP. *See, e.g., Carson Harbor Village v. County of Los Angeles*, 433 F.3d 1260 (9th Cir. 2006); *Union Pacific R. Co. v. Reilly Indus., Inc.*, 215 F.3d 830 (8th Cir. 2000). The NCP itself defines when a nongovernmental response action should be considered "consistent with the NCP." Under 40 C.F.R. § 300.700(c)(3)(i), nongovernmental response actions that EPA has neither selected nor supervised will be considered consistent with the NCP if, when evaluated as a whole, those actions are in "substantial compliance with applicable requirements" and result in a "CERCLA-quality cleanup." The "applicable requirements" of the NCP that private parties must follow to recover their response costs include NCP provisions that concern the selection and implementation of response actions and requirements concerning both public participation and worker safety. *Id.*

3. Natural Resource Damages

Under CERCLA, responsible parties are liable for injury to, destruction of, or loss of natural resources, including the reasonable costs of assessing such injury, destruction, or loss resulting from a hazardous substance release. CERCLA § 107(a)(4)(C), 42 U.S.C. § 9607(a)(4)(C). The term "natural resources" is defined in the Act as "land, fish, biota, air, water, ground water, drinking water supplies, and other resources belonging to, managed by, held in trust by, appertaining to, or otherwise controlled by the United States. . . . any State or local government . . . foreign nation . . . [or] Indian tribe." CERCLA § 101(16), 42 U.S.C. § 9601(16). Under the statute, natural resource damage ("NRD") claims are limited to governmental natural resources trustees, i.e., Federal, State, local, or Indian tribe agencies or officials that own, manage, regulate, or otherwise control natural resources that have been injured, lost or destroyed. *Id.* Purely private property is excluded from CERCLA's definition of natural resources. *See Ohio v. U.S. Department of Interior*, 880 F.2d 432 (D.C. Cir. 1989).

Trustees who recover natural resource damages are entitled to retain and use them, rather than depositing them in the general Treasury. However, the proceeds from a successful NRD lawsuit may only be used "to restore, replace, or acquire the equivalent of" the damaged or lost natural resources in question.

NRD litigation often involves sharp disputes over the extent of the harm to, and lost use of, natural resources, as well as the quantification of damages. With respect to the latter, the U.S. Department of Interior promulgated rules of natural resource damage assessments that set out the methods that natural resource trustees may use to estimate the extent of injury to, loss of, or destruction of natural resources resulting from a release of hazardous substances, and to monetize the resulting damages. *See* 43 C.F.R. pt. 11. Although nominally "not mandatory," natural resource trustees generally rely on those regulations because CERCLA provides that an assessment of damages to natural resources made by a Federal or State trustee within the regulations "shall have the force of a rebuttable presumption on behalf of the trustee in any administrative or judicial proceeding." CERCLA § 107(f)(2)(C), 42 U.S.C. § 9607(f)(2)(C).

4. *Health Assessment Costs*

The Agency for Toxic Substances and Disease Registry (ATSDR), a federal agency created by CERCLA, is required to conduct a health assessment for every facility listed on the NPL. CERCLA §§ 104(i)(6)(A) and (B), 42 U.S.C. §§ 9604(i)(6)(A) and (B). The ATSDR is also authorized to conduct such a health assessment for other hazardous substance releases. *Id.* And, where warranted, the ATSDR may also conduct a full-scale epidemiological study of the health effects of the release of hazardous substances on an exposed population. Responsible parties are liable for "the costs of any health assessment or health effects study" carried out by the ATSDR. CERCLA § 107(a)(4)(D), 42 U.S.C. § 9607(a)(4)(D). These costs, however, are rarely in dispute in Superfund cost-recovery cases since they are typically relatively small compared with other government response costs.

D. The Liability of Multiple Responsible Parties

Superfund cases very often involve more than one responsible party. Given this, questions often arise as to the scope of liability. Courts must decide whether all of the defendants will be held jointly and severally liable—allowing the plaintiff (at least in theory) to recover the full amount of the liability from any single defendant—or severally liable, making each defendant responsible for only a share of the claim.

In fashioning the compromise that led to the initial enactment of CERCLA in 1981, Congress intentionally reserved this important issue for determination by the federal courts. Senator Randolph, a co-sponsor of the bill, stated during the congressional debate that preceded the enactment of the statute, "[W]e have deleted any reference to joint and several liability, relying on common law principles to determine when parties should be severally liable." Randolph also told his colleagues on the floor of the Senate that "it is intended that issues of liability not resolved by this act, if any, shall be governed by traditional and evolving principles of common law."

In the early days of the Superfund program, the scope-of-liability question was authoritatively resolved by the widely cited opinion of Chief Judge Rubin in the seminal case of *United States v. Chem Dyne Corp.*, 572 F. Supp. 802 (S.D. Ohio 1983). After reviewing the pertinent portions of CERCLA's legislative history, Judge Rubin reasoned that because Superfund is a federal program implicating the "rights, liabilities, and responsibilities of the United States," the liability features of the Act are appropriate for uniform national treatment by the judiciary. Thus, he determined, federal common law—rather than the diverse substantive rules of individual States—should apply. *Id.*

To find the "evolving principles of common law" that pertain to Superfund liability, the *Chem Dyne* court looked to Sections 433A and 875 of the Restatement (2d) of Torts. Under that broadly accepted formula, where two or more persons cause a single and indivisible harm, each of them is jointly and severally liable. However, where two or more persons acting independently cause a distinct or single harm, for which there is "a reasonable basis for division according to the contribution of each," each such person is severally liable only for the portion of the harm that person has caused. *Id.* And each defendant has the burden of proof with regard to apportionment. *Id.*

Numerous federal district courts, and every U.S. Circuit Court of Appeals that considered the issue, adopted Judge Rubin's analysis in *Chem Dyne. See, e.g., United States v. R.W. Meyer, Inc.*, 889 F.2d 1497 (6th Cir. 1989); *United States v. Monsanto Co., supra.* Nonetheless, following *Chem Dyne*, a question remained as to precisely what defendants in CERCLA enforcement cases had to prove in order to demonstrate that apportionment of damages was called for.

Most multiparty Superfund cases involve facilities at which hazardous substances have mixed, or "comingled," into a sort of toxic soup. Federal courts have typically rejected government contentions that all comingled sites are *per se* instances of single, indivisible harm. *See, e.g., United States v. Alcan Aluminum Co.*, 964 F.2d 252 (3d Cir. 1992). Nonetheless, the courts have erected substantial evidentiary obstacles to defendants who wish to demonstrate divisibility of harm at contaminated facilities. Thus, it has been held that where hazardous substances have comingled, each defendant must introduce evidence of the mobility, toxicity, and interactive characteristics of the hazardous substances contributed by each defendant, along with the volume of hazardous substances that each has contributed, to demonstrate a reasonable basis for apportioning liability. *See, e.g., United States v. Monsanto Co., supra*. Moreover, courts have insisted on "concrete and specific evidence" of the divisibility of harm, even in cases where they have found that the harm at a facility may be reasonably apportioned. *United States v. Hercules, Inc.*, 247 F.3d 706 (8th Cir. 2001).

Notwithstanding these formidable evidentiary hurdles, however, defendants have succeeded in proving divisibility of harm in a small number of CERCLA cases. One example is *United States v. Bell Petroleum Servs.*, 3 F.3d 889 (5th Cir. 1983), where the court imposed several liability based on the length of time each defendant operated the same facility, in a situation where three businesses successively operated the same facility in the same way, and released the same single hazardous substance into the environment. In a more celebrated opinion, a divided U.S. Supreme Court reversed a decision of the Ninth Circuit and reinstated a U.S. District Court opinion that applied a complex formula—based on the total area of a contaminated facility and two other factors—to conclude that CERCLA liability at the hazardous substance facility in question must be apportioned among several parties. *Burlington Northern and Santa Fe Railway Co. v. United States, supra.*

Thus far, however, the lower federal courts have often failed to follow *Burlington Northern* in subsequent CERCLA cases. *See, e.g., United States v. NCR Corp.*, 688 F.3d 833 (7th Cir. 2012). *See also* Steve C. Gold, *Disjointed? Several Approaches to Divisibility after* Burlington Northern, 11 Vt. J. Envtl. L. 307 (2009). Thus, it still appears accurate to observe, as the U.S. Court of Appeals for the First Circuit did in 1989, that "the practical effect of placing the burden on defendants has been that responsible parties rarely escape joint and several liability." *O'Neil v. Picillo*, 883 F.2d 176 (1st Cir. 1989).

E. Contribution and Private Party Cost Recovery Actions

As amended in 1986, CERCLA provides a cause of action for contribution to any person against "any person who is liable or potentially liable [under § 107(a)] during or following any civil action under [§ 106] or under [§ 107(a)]." CERCLA § 113(f)(1), 42 U.S.C. § 9613(f)(1). This provision of the Act essentially adopts a common law doctrine allowing jointly and severally liable parties, aggrieved because they have allegedly paid more than their "fair share" of a common liability, to recover from other liable parties any additional shares of the money paid by the contribution-action-plaintiff to the plaintiff in the original lawsuit. The statute gives little specific guidance to courts with regard to how to determine the appropriate share of liability to allocate to each party. It merely provides that "in resolving contribution claims, the court may allocate response costs among liable parties using such equitable factors as the court determines are appropriate." *Id.*

Many courts have found it helpful to apply six separate factors—the so-called "Gore factors"—in ruling on CERCLA contribution claims. These factors are: (i) the ability of the parties to demonstrate that their contribution to a discharge, release, or disposal of waste can be distinguished; (ii) the amount of hazardous substances involved; (iii) the degree of toxicity of those substances; (iv) the degree of involvement by the parties in the generation, transportation, treatment, storage or disposal of the hazardous substances; (v) the degree of care exercised by the parties with respect to the hazardous substances in question; and (vi) the degree to which the parties have cooperated with government officials to prevent any harm to public health or the environment. While not universally adopted, these variables have been widely applied by the courts in CERCLA contribution matters.

One question that has arisen is which parties are entitled to pursue CERCLA contribution claims. The U.S. Supreme Court resolved that question by holding that to be eligible to sue another party in a contribution action, a plaintiff must have either been sued by a governmental entity under CERCLA sections 106 or 107, or entered into a settlement with a government requiring the payment of response costs. *Cooper Industries, Inc. v. Aviall Services, Inc.*, 543 U.S. 157 (2004).

The *Cooper Industries* decision left open the issue of whether a responsible party who is barred from bringing a CERCLA contribution case may instead institute a cost recovery action under § 107 of the statute. The Supreme Court subsequently answered that question in the affirmative in *United States v. Atlantic Research Corp.*, 551 U.S. 128 (2007). The Court ruled that any person other than the United States, a State, or an Indian tribe, may recover any money it has expended to clean up a contaminated facility without having first been the target of a CERCLA enforcement action.

CERCLA encourages the prompt settlement of governmental claims against PRPs. However, the statute does impose some substantial limitations and procedures with respect to settlements. The most significant of these requirements involve settlements in which responsible parties agree to conduct remedial actions. First, with regard to RI/FSs, EPA may not delegate their preparation to PRPs unless they are "qualified to conduct the RI/FS."

And the Agency must ensure that a "qualified person" oversees and reviews the preparation of that document. CERCLA § 104(a)(1), 42 U.S.C. § 9604(a)(1). Second, settlements calling for PRP performance of an RI/FS may not contain any general releases of liability. Instead, settling defendants may only be granted a covenant not to sue, conditioned on satisfactory performance of the remedial action, that includes a "reopener provision" if it is later determined that the originally selected remedy is not sufficiently protective of human health or the environment. CERCLA § 122(f), 42 U.S.C. § 9622(f). Remedial settlements must also include stipulated penalties where settling defendants failed to perform their agreed-upon obligations. And settlement agreements must be in the form of a judicial consent decree, subjected to public notice and comment, and later approved by the court.

In deciding whether to approve or reject consent decrees in Superfund remedial matters, courts tend to defer to government estimates of litigation risk and settlement strategies. To gain judicial approval, courts must find that the settlement is fair, reasonable, and faithful to the goals of the statute. *United States v. Cannons Engineering Corp.*, 899 F.2d 79 (1st Cir. 1990). Moreover, appellate courts will typically defer to the decisions of trial judges in these cases unless they reflect a "manifest abuse of discretion." *See, e.g.*, *United States v. Charles George Trucking, Inc.*, 34 F.3d 1081 (1st Cir. 1994).

Checkpoints

- EPA's response action process has multiple steps, including:
    - Preliminary assessment/site investigation at a reportedly contaminated hazardous substance facility.
    - A short-term "removal action" (if necessary).
    - Assessment of risk through a standard "hazard ranking system."
    - Listing on the National Priorities List for remedial action (where appropriate).
    - Preparation of a remedial investigation/feasibility study.
    - Selection of a cleanup remedy that is memorialized in a Record of Decision.
    - Design and implementation of a remedial design/remedial action.
    - Delisting of the facility from the National Priorities List.
    - Continued operation and maintenance activities at the facility (where needed).
- CERCLA creates potential liability for four categories of parties:
    - Present owners or operators of hazardous substance facilities.
    - Past owners or operators of facilities at which hazardous substances were disposed during their period of ownership or operation.
    - Parties that arranged for disposal or treatment of their hazardous substances by another.
    - Persons who accepted hazardous substances for transport to facilities or incineration sites from which there is a hazardous substance release.
- PRPs may be liable for:
    - Response costs incurred by government entities.
    - Response costs of nongovernment parties.
    - Natural resource damages.
    - Health assessment costs.
- In most cases, PRPs are strictly, joint and severally, and retroactively liable for cleanup costs, particularly (though not exclusively) where different hazardous substances have comingled at contaminated facilities.
- In a small minority of cases, PRPs have succeeded in avoiding joint and several liability by proving the divisibility of harm at hazardous substance facilities.
- CERCLA provides a cause of action for contribution for jointly and severally liable PRPs who seek to recover a fairer share of a common liability from other PRPs.

- Courts allocate response costs in contribution suits based upon whatever equitable factors the courts deem appropriate.
- Parties may only sue other parties for contribution where they have themselves been subject to a government enforcement action, or entered into a settlement with a government entity.
- In circumstances where it has not been subject to government enforcement action, any nongovernmental party may recover any money it has expended to clean up a contaminated facility under a separate provision of CERCLA that does not create a statutory right to contribution.
- CERCLA imposes certain substantial and procedural limitations with respect to settlements in remedial actions:
    - Only qualified persons may be permitted to prepare remedial investigation/feasibility studies.
    - Settlements calling for PRP performance of remedial actions may not contain general releases of liability.
    - PRPs may be granted covenants not to sue, subject to "re-opener provisions."
    - Remedial settlements must include stipulated penalties where agreed-upon obligations are not fulfilled by PRPs.
    - Settlement agreements must be in the form of a Consent Decree, to be approved by a federal judge following public notice and comment.
- Courts will typically approve consent decrees in CERCLA remedial cases where the settlement is fair, reasonable, and faithful to the goals of the statute.

Chapter 6

The Resource Conservation and Recovery Act

Roadmap

- Understand the regulation of non-hazardous solid waste.
- Learn how "solid waste" and "hazardous waste" are defined and identified.
- Be able to grasp the requirements that apply to hazardous waste and generators and transporters, and to facilities that treat, store, and dispose of hazardous waste.
- Understand the relative roles of federal and state agencies in administering RCRA.
- Learn how the statute is enforced by federal officials, state agencies, and private citizens.

I. Introduction

The Resource Conservation and Recovery Act ("RCRA") is an important federal statute that has two primary purposes: improving the disposal of non-hazardous solid waste (such as household trash and yard cuttings) and requiring "cradle-to-grave" management of hazardous waste (such as benzene and trichloroethylene). Like other federal environmental statutes, the Act calls upon the U.S. Environmental Protection Agency ("EPA" or "the Agency") to develop and implement regulations that will accomplish both purposes. The second of these goals, however, has proven time-consuming, technically complex, and controversial for EPA. Nonetheless, after a slow start and a sharp prod from Congress—which passed a stringent set of amendments to the act in 1984, reflecting congressional dissatisfaction with the agency's initial performance in developing and implementing a comprehensive program to regulate hazardous waste—EPA ultimately promulgated technical guidelines for state regulation of non-hazardous solid wastes and created voluminous, detailed regulations regarding hazardous waste management.

The remainder of this chapter illuminates the approaches EPA has taken to comply with Congress's demanding legislative directives. We will first consider the Agency's non-hazardous solid waste guidelines for state programs to prohibit open dumping and substitute safer waste disposal practices. We'll then turn to EPA's regulations concerning hazardous wastes. In particular, we will focus on EPA regulations concerning the definition and identification of hazardous waste materials, the Agency's rules pertaining to generators and disposers of such waste, and the tools available to government agencies and private citizens for enforcing hazardous waste requirements.

II. Regulation of Non-Hazardous Solid Wastes under RCRA Subtitle D

Americans generate vast amounts of municipal solid waste—258 million tons in 2014 according to EPA. Our trash includes a wide variety of items, including uneaten food, packaging, grass clippings, sofas, tires, refrigerators, computers and other materials. Although slightly more than one-third of this non-hazardous waste is now recycled or composted, a majority of it is disposed of in municipal solid waste landfills.

Subtitle D of RCRA mainly focuses on what occurs at those local landfills. The statute prohibits the depositing of wastes in "open dumps," which are defined as any facility or site that is neither a "sanitary landfill" nor a facility for the disposal of hazardous waste. *See* RCRA § 1004(14), 42 U.S.C. § 6903(14) and RCRA § 4005(a), 42 U.S.C. § 6945(a). "Sanitary landfills," in turn, are facilities that satisfy EPA-established criteria so that "there is no reasonable probability of adverse effects on health or the environment from disposal of solid waste at such [facilities]." RCRA § 4004(a), 42 U.S.C. § 6944(a). EPA has issued detailed, technical criteria for municipal solid waste landfills. *See* 40 C.F.R. pt. 258. The Agency's criteria for other types of non-hazardous waste landfills are codified at 40 C.F.R. pt. 257.

RCRA contemplates that the collection and disposal of solid waste is to take place at the state and local level, with guidance and assistance from EPA. Under Subtitle D, individual states are required to develop their own solid waste management plans that are to be submitted to EPA for approval. *See* RCRA §§ 4002, 4003, 4004(b), and 4006, 42 U.S.C. §§ 6942, 6943, 6944(b), and 6946. The Agency must approve these plans as long as they meet certain requirements, including the ban on all open dumps referred to above. At least 38 states, two U.S. territories, and one Indian tribe have now received full or partial EPA approval to run their own solid waste programs.

III. Regulation of Hazardous Waste under RCRA Subtitle C

Subtitle C of RCRA is meant to protect human health and the environment from dangers posed by the unsafe handling and disposal of hazardous waste. It directs EPA to establish requirements for three types of participants in the lifecycle of hazardous waste: generators, transporters, and owners and operators of treatment, storage, and disposal facilities ("TSDFs"). EPA's regulations set out how generators, transporters and TSDFs must handle hazardous waste and what records they must keep to track the creation, transport, and disposition of such waste. They also detail the corrective actions that must be taken where hazardous waste is released to the environment; and they indicate how states may obtain authorization to run hazardous waste programs.

A. Defining and Identifying Hazardous Waste

RCRA directed EPA to "develop and promulgate criteria for identifying the characteristics of hazardous waste, and for listing hazardous waste . . . taking into account toxicity, persistence, and degradability in nature, potential for accumulation in tissue, and other related factors such as flammability, corrosiveness, and other hazardous characteristics." RCRA § 3001(a), 42 U.S.C. § 6921(a). The Act also defines the term "hazardous waste" to some extent, stating that it means "a solid waste, or combination of solid wastes, which because of its quantity, concentration, or physical, chemical, or infectious characteristics may (A) cause, or significantly contribute to an increase in mortality or an increase in serious irreversible, or incapacitating reversible illness; or (B) pose a substantial present or potential hazard to human health or the environment when improperly treated, stored, transported, or disposed of, or otherwise managed." RCRA § 1004(5), 42 U.S.C. § 6903(5). Thus, it must be noted, to qualify as hazardous, a waste must first be a solid waste or combination of solid wastes.

1. When Is a Waste a "Solid Waste"?

The statute provides a specific definition of "solid waste." It states that "[t]he term "solid waste" means "any garbage, refuse, sludge from a waste treatment plant, or air pollution control facility and other discarded material, including solid, liquid, semi-solid, or contained gaseous material resulting from industrial, commercial, mining, and agricultural operations, and from community activities[.]" RCRA § 1004(27), 42 U.S.C. § 6903(27). This definition also identifies certain types of waste streams that are excluded from the solid waste category because they are regulated under other federal environmental statutes. It thus provides that the term solid waste "does not include solid or dissolved material in domestic sewage, or solid or dissolved materials in irrigation return flows or industrial discharges which are point sources subject to permits under section 1342 of Title 33, or source, special nuclear, or byproduct material as defined by the Atomic Energy Act of 1954, as amended. . . ." *Id.*

RCRA's solid waste definition thus makes clear that "solid waste" includes a range of types of matter generated by a variety of types of human activities. Counterintuitively, a solid waste need not be solid. Instead, it may consist of "solid, liquid, semi-solid, or contained gaseous material." Similarly, a material may fit the definition of solid waste whether it came from industrial, commercial, mining, agricultural, or community sources.

RCRA also indicates that to be a solid waste a material must be "discarded." This term is somewhat ambiguous and has led to confusion and controversy. Where a pesticide is sprayed into the air over land and water, has it been discarded within the meaning of RCRA? The Second Circuit held that the answer is no, since the pesticide spraying in issue was a purposeful activity, aimed at reaching and killing disease-carrying mosquitoes and their larvae. *See No Spray Coalition, Inc. v. City of New York*, 252 F.3d 148 (2d Cir. 2001). In contrast, however, the U.S. Circuit Court of Appeals for the Second Circuit has also held that spent lead shot and clay targets from a shooting range constituted solid waste under the statutory definition. *Connecticut Coastal Fisherman's Assn. v. Remington Arms Co., Inc.*, 989 F.2d 1305 (2d Cir. 1993).

EPA has established a regulatory definition of discarded materials that has been revised a number of times since its first iteration. (*See* 40 C.F.R. § 261.2 for the most recent definition.) Under the Agency's current regulatory approach, materials are considered discarded if they have been abandoned, are considered "inherently waste-like," have been accumulated in an excessive manner before being legitimately recycled, or have been "sham recycled."

EPA deems a material to be legitimately recycled if it is "used, reused, or reclaimed," and it provides a useful contribution to a recycling process that produces a valuable output. 40 C.F.R §§ 261.1(c)(7) and 260.42. Sham recycling, in contrast, involves using more material than is necessary to produce the output, or using material to produce a useless or ineffective output. The latter is considered a type of "abandonment," and materials that are sham recycled are thus viewed as solid wastes. 40 C.F.R. § 261.2(b)(4) and (g).

2. *When Is a "Solid Waste" Also a "Hazardous Waste"?*

a. Characteristic and Listed Hazardous Wastes

EPA's subtitle C regulations established two ways that a solid waste will be considered a "hazardous waste": by having one or more hazardous characteristics ("characteristic hazardous wastes") or by being specifically listed as a hazardous waste by EPA ("listed hazardous wastes").

Characteristic hazardous wastes are wastes with measurable properties indicating that the waste can cause death or injury to humans or lead to ecological damage. EPA established standards for hazardous waste characteristics that can be detected by use of a standardized test method: ignitability, reactivity, corrosivity, and toxicity.

The ignitability characteristic identifies waste that can readily catch fire and sustain combustion, such as paints, cleaners, and other industrial wastes. *See* 40 C.F.R. § 261.21. Corrosive hazardous wastes, such as automobile batteries, are waste materials that are acidic (or, in some case, alkaline) and that can readily corrode or dissolve metal, flesh, or other materials. *See* 40 C.F.R. § 261.22. The reactivity characteristic identifies wastes that readily explode or undergo violent reactions, or react with other chemicals to release toxic gases or fumes. *See* 40 C.F.R. § 261.23. In contrast, waste materials with the toxicity characteristic are wastes likely to leach dangerous concentrations of toxic chemicals into groundwater. EPA has designed a lab procedure, known as the Toxicity Characteristic Leaching Procedure ("TCLP"), to estimate the leaching potential of waste when disposing a municipal solid waste landfill. This procedure requires waste generators to create a liquid leachate from its hazardous waste samples that must be analyzed to determine whether they contain any of 40 toxic chemicals in concentrations that exceed specified regulatory levels. Where that is shown to be the case, those wastes are considered toxic characteristic wastes. *See* 40 C.F.R. § 261.24.

To guide its decision-making regarding which wastes should be listed as hazardous, EPA developed a set of three criteria. These criteria ask whether: (i) the waste typically contains toxic chemicals that could pose a threat to human health or the environment if improperly managed ("toxic listed wastes"); (ii) the waste is fatal to humans and animals even in low doses, and thus could pose a threat to human health or the environment even if properly managed ("acute hazardous wastes"); and/or (iii) the waste typically exhibits one or more of the four specific characteristics of hazardous waste discussed above (ignitability, corrosivity, reactivity, and toxicity). Once identified by EPA as hazardous, the wastes in question are included on one of four lists promulgated in the *Federal Register* and assigned a waste code for purposes of identification. *See* 40 C.F.R. §§ 261.31, 261.32, and 261.33.

Listed and characteristic categories of hazardous wastes are not mutually exclusive. Thus, a given waste may be specifically listed and also constitute a characteristic hazardous waste if it is ignitable, corrosive, reactive, or toxic as EPA has defined that characteristic and the testing procedures to be used to identify them.

b. The Mixture and Derived-From Rules

In order to prevent generators from evading RCRA Subtitle C requirements by comingling listed hazardous wastes with non-hazardous solid waste, EPA established a rule, generally referred to as "the mixture rule," that provides that waste mixtures containing listed hazardous wastes are to be regulated as hazardous waste—regardless of the actual hazardous properties of the mixture or the proportion of hazardous to non-hazardous waste contained in the mixture. 40 C.F.R. § 261.3(a)(2)(iv). EPA's regulations also defined as hazardous waste any solid waste "derived from" listed hazardous waste, i.e., solid waste that was generated by the storage, disposal, and treatment of a listed waste. *Id.* These rules were upheld on judicial review, even though, in some instances, these mixtures and derived-from wastes may not present the kinds of hazards that RCRA and its regulations were designed to prevent. *See American Chemistry Council v. EPA*, 337 F.3d 1060 (D.C. Cir. 2003).

3. Exclusions from RCRA Hazardous Waste Regulation

EPA's regulations identify 17 hazardous wastes as excluded from the RCRA Subtitle C regulatory scheme. 40 C.F.R. § 261.4(b). The two most significant of these exclusions are the household waste exclusion and the exclusion of certain wastes from mining and mineral processing.

Under the Agency's regulations, "household waste, including household waste that has been collected, transported, stored, treated, disposed, recovered . . . or reused," is outside the definition of hazardous waste. 40 C.F.R. § 261.4(b). "Household waste" is specifically defined as "any material (including garbage, trash, and sanitary wastes in septic tanks) derived from households (including single and multiple residences, hotels and motels, bunk houses, ranger stations, crew quarters, campgrounds, picnic grounds, and day-use recreation areas)." 40 C.F.R. § 264.1(b)(1).

Unfortunately, much household waste does contain discarded materials that are hazardous in nature. Some examples include mothballs, paints, solvents, mercury-containing thermometers, batteries, drain openers and insecticides. Nonetheless, EPA recognized that subjecting household wastes to strict RCRA waste management regulations would create numerous practical problems. It thus interpreted RCRA as reflecting a congressional intent to exclude those wastes from Subtitle C regulation.

The extraction and processing of usable minerals from the earth generates truly immense volumes of waste materials, a number of which are hazardous. Regulating these wastes in the same manner as other hazardous wastes would create serious problems of cost and practicality. As a result, Congress explicitly provided EPA with the authority to modify various of the subtitle C standards for hazardous waste disposal to take account of the special characteristics of mining wastes, including "the practical difficulties associated with implementation of such requirements, and site specific characteristics, including but not limited to the climate, geology, hydrology, and soil chemistry at the site. . . ." RCRA § 3004(x), 42 U.S.C. § 6924(x).

EPA's current set of regulations exclude from the definition of hazardous waste nearly all solid waste generated by the extraction and "beneficiation" (i.e., preparation for smelting) of ores and minerals. 40 C.F.R. § 261.4(b)(7)(ii)(A).

IV. Implementation of RCRA Subtitle C

A. Requirements for Hazardous Waste Generators

EPA's RCRA regulations define a "generator" as "any person, by site, whose act produces hazardous waste . . . or whose act first causes a hazardous waste to be subject to regulation." 40 C.F.R. § 260.10. The statute directs EPA to establish standards for generators regarding hazardous waste containers and their labels, and for the "use of a manifest system and any other reasonable means necessary to assure that all hazardous waste generated is designated for treatment, storage, or disposal in, and arrives at, treatment, storage, or disposal facilities (other than facilities on the premises where the waste is generated) for which a permit has been issued. . . ." RCRA § 3002(a)(5), 42 U.S.C. § 6922(a)(5). The "manifest" document is defined in the statute as "a form used for identifying the quantity, composition, and the origin, routing, and destination of hazardous waste during its transportation from the point of generation to the point of disposal, treatment, or storage." *Id.* It is designed to ensure that hazardous waste reaches its intended destination, or else to inform governmental authorities whenever hazardous waste does not end up in a permitted treatment, storage, or disposal facility.

EPA's regulations establishing standards for hazardous waste generators can be found at 40 C.F.R. pt. 262; and its specific requirements for hazardous waste manifests are located at 40 C.F.R. §§262.20 to 262.27. Under those regulations, the obligations of generators vary with the amount of hazardous waste they generate in a given month. EPA has created three size categories of generators: large quantity, small quantity, and very small quantity. Not surprisingly, the requirements for large quantity generators are more stringent than those that apply to small quantity generators. Very small quantity generators are exempt from most RCRA hazardous waste generator requirements, though they must still properly characterize and label their wastes and they must have their hazardous waste treated or disposed of at a permitted facility. 40 C.F.R. §262.14.

As a practical matter, generators must generally hold onto their hazardous wastes before shipping them off-site. However, if they store them for too long a time, their facilities become subject to the stringent requirements applicable to treatment, storage, or disposal facilities discussed below. As a result, EPA allows generators to accumulate certain amounts of hazardous wastes for limited periods without engaging in the "storage" of those wastes. The allowable accumulation limitations and periods vary, depending upon whether the generators in question are classified as large, small, or very small quantity generators.

B. Requirements for Transporters of Hazardous Waste

RCRA directed EPA to promulgate regulations applicable to transporters of hazardous waste, RCRA §3003, 42 U.S.C. §6923, and the Agency did so. *See* 40 C.F.R. pt. 263. Transporters, like generators, are subject to recordkeeping requirements. They must use the manifest document that the generator prepared to track each shipment of hazardous waste, and they must comply with the instructions in the manifest by bringing the hazardous waste to the destination that the generator has designated. 40 C.F.R. §§263.20 and 263.21. In addition, should a spill occur during hazardous waste transportation, EPA's regulations require transporters to immediately notify government authorities, and to take immediate steps to clean up the spilled materials and protect human health and the environment. 40 C.F.R. §§263.30 and 263.31.

C. Requirements Concerning Treatment, Storage, and Disposal Facilities (TSDFs)

1. *Key Definitions and the Scope of the Regulations*

RCRA directs EPA to promulgate "performance standards" for treatment, storage, and disposal facilities (TSDFs), and to establish "regulations requiring each person owning or operating an existing [TSDF] or planning to construct a new [TSDF] ... to have a permit...." RCRA § 3005(a), 42 U.S.C. § 6925(a). The statute provides definitions of the terms "disposal," "storage," and "treatment." *See* RCRA § 1004, 42 U.S.C. § 6903. However, to clarify the meaning of those statutory definitions, and make them easier to apply and enforce in practice, EPA promulgated its own regulatory definitions of the same terms.

As EPA has broadly defined it, "treatment" means "any method, technique, or process, including neutralization, designed to change the physical, chemical or biological character or composition of any hazardous waste so as to neutralize such waste, or so as to recover energy of material resources from the waste, or so as to render such waste non-hazardous or less hazardous; safer to transport, store or dispose of; or amenable for recovery, amenable for storage, or reduced in volume." 40 C.F.R. §§ 260.10 and 270.2. "Storage," according to the regulations, is "the holding of hazardous waste for a temporary period, at the end of which the hazardous waste is treated, disposed of, or stored elsewhere." 40 C.F.R. §§ 260.10 and 270.2.

The regulatory definition of "disposal" simply repeats the statutory definition of that word, with the sole exception of the elimination of the phrase "solid waste." Thus, for purposes of RCRA TSDF permitting, "disposal" connotes "the deposit, injection, dumping, spilling, leaking or placing of any hazardous waste into or on any land or water so that such hazardous waste ... may enter the environment or be emitted into the air or discharged into any waters, including ground waters." *See* RCRA § 1004(3), 42 U.S.C. § 6903(3) and 40 C.F.R. § 270.2. A "disposal facility" means "a facility, or part of a facility, at which hazardous waste is intentionally placed into or on the land or water, at which hazardous waste will remain after closure...." 40 C.F.R. §§ 260.10 and 270.2. And, for purposes of the RCRA regulatory program, the terms "owner" and "operator" are defined thusly: "Operator means the person responsible for the overall operation of a facility. Owner means the person who owns the facility or part of a facility." 40 C.F.R. § 260.10.

2. *TSDF Permit Requirements*

Under RCRA, persons who own, operate, or plan to construct a new TSDF must obtain a permit to do so. RCRA § 3005(a), 42 U.S.C. § 6925(a). Permits provide TSDF owners and operators with legal authority to treat, store, and dispose of hazardous waste. They also detail how the facility must comply with applicable regulations.

Facilities that were in existence prior to the enactment of RCRA were allowed to stay in operation in an "interim status," as long as they made application for a permit and complied with EPA's regulatory requirements for interim status facilities. *See* RCRA §3005(e), 42 U.S.C. §6925(e), and 40 C.F.R. part 265. Interim status standards are somewhat less stringent than the standards that apply to fully permitted TSDFs. Interim status continues while the facility's owner or operator's permit application is pending; and it ends when the application is granted or denied.

Applications for RCRA permits for TSDFs consist of two parts: A and B. Though the Part A application is relatively brief and straightforward, the second application part ("Part B") is lengthy and detailed, and requires a significant investment of time and money. In a Part B application, considerable information must be submitted regarding the facility (or proposed facility), analyses of the hazardous waste to be handled there, contingency plans in the event of spills, upsets, or equipment failures, training procedures, and topographic maps, along with other, specific information that pertains to the particular type of unit in question.

Once a Part B permit application is filed, a dialogue is begun between the TSDF owner or operator and government officials to iron out the specific terms of the permit. These negotiations are open to the public, and members of the public may also actively participate in the permitting process. *See* 40 C.F.R. pt. 124, Subparts A and B.

3. *Regulating the Operation of TSDFs*

When RCRA was amended in 1984, Congress added a significant number of provisions requiring EPA to prescribe performance standards for TSDFs. These provisions establish requirements for particular types of hazardous wastes, different types of disposal facilities and disposal methods, types of treatment, and other matters. RCRA §3004(b)–(y), 42 U.S.C. §6924(b)–(y). EPA responded to these mandates by promulgating extensive TSDF regulations. The Agency's rules include both requirements that specifically address subjects listed in the statute and regulations pertaining to particular kinds of treatment, storage, or disposal units (TSDFs). *See generally* 40 C.F.R. pt. 264, Subparts B–E.

Owners and operators of TSDFs must test incoming wastes to confirm that they are as described in the manifest document that accompanied the wastes. 40 C.F.R. §264.13(a)(1). They must return a copy of the manifest to the generator of the hazardous waste in question, submit periodic reports to government regulators, and keep a copy of the manifest for themselves.

TSDF owners and operators must also plan to prevent and respond to emergencies, ensure that their employees meet training requirements, and keep separate from one another wastes that, if mixed, would create risks of fire or explosion. 40 C.F.R. pt. 264, Subparts B–E; and 40 C.F.R. § 264.17.

EPA's Subtitle C regulations also create detailed technical requirements that vary by type of hazardous waste, hazardous waste management facility, and "unit" within such a facility (e.g., containers, landfills, tanks, waste piles, etc.). *See* 40 C.F.R. pt. 264, Subparts I–EE, and pt. 266. In general, these rules require that units holding hazardous waste be designed, constructed, operated, and maintained to prevent the release of hazardous waste into any environmental medium. They also require TSDFs to build secondary containment structures (such as double walls on tanks and double liners under landfill units) that will capture any hazardous waste spills or leaks.

4. Land Disposal Regulations

In 1984, Congress amended RCRA to make land disposal the least favored method for managing hazardous wastes. *See* RCRA § 3004(b)–(m), 42 U.S.C. § 5924(b)–(m). EPA was required to promulgate regulations "specifying those levels or methods of treatment, if any, which substantially diminish the toxicity of the waste or substantially reduce the likelihood of migration of hazardous constituents from the waste so that short-term and long-term threats to human health and the environment are minimized." RCRA § 3004(m), 42 U.S.C. § 6924(m). EPA's corresponding regulations—commonly referred to as "the land ban"—prohibit the land disposal of hazardous waste unless it is first treated (without being diluted) to attain concentrations of hazardous constituents that are below standards established in the regulations. 40 C.F.R. § 268.1 and 268.3. These regulations reflect a conclusion by the Agency that "land treatment" should not be considered a permissible treatment technology. That premise was upheld by the D.C. Circuit, which rejected an argument by several trade associations that EPA should have permitted land treatment as the sort of "best demonstrated available technology" that the Agency's regulations expressly encourage. *See American Petroleum Inst. v. EPA*, 906 F.2d 729 (D.C. Cir. 1990).

5. Corrective Action Requirements

RCRA provides that all TSDF permits shall require "corrective action" for all releases of hazardous waste from any solid waste management unit at the permitted TSDF. RCRA § 3004(u), 42 U.S.C. § 6924(u). "Corrective action" must be taken "where necessary to protect human health and the environment," even when such action is needed beyond the boundary of the facility itself. RCRA § 3004(v), 42 U.S.C. § 6924(v).

TSDF permits thus contain affirmative requirements that facility owners or operators undertake measures to clean up all releases of hazardous waste. These cleanup activities must meet the standard of protectiveness prescribed by the statute.

In contrast to most of its other regulations applicable to TSDFs, EPA's corrective action rules tend to be general and procedural rather than prescriptive. This reflects the Agency's understanding that conditions at individual facilities vary widely, and individual corrective action choices must be tailored to those conditions. *See* 40 C.F.R. §§264.100 and 264.101.

6. TSDF Closure and Post-Closure Requirements

EPA's Subtitle C regulations impose stringent requirements for safe closure and post-closure care of TSDFs. Closure and post-closure plans for such facilities, along with documentation of financial assurance, must be included in the facilities' Part B permit applications. 40 C.F.R. §270.14(13) and 15–18. Owners and operators of TSDFs must close their facilities "in a manner that minimizes the need for further maintenance and controls, [and] minimizes or eliminates, to the extent necessary to protect human health and the environment, post-closure escape of hazardous waste. . . ." 40 C.F.R. §264.111. TSDF owners and operators must also provide assurance that sufficient funds will be available to implement their closure and post-closure plans. This assurance must be accomplished through one of a number of prescribed financial mechanisms such as insurance policies, surety bonds, trust funds, and letters of credit. 40 C.F.R. §264.140–264.151.

D. The Role of the States in RCRA Implementation

As is the case with other federal environmental legislation, states have a critical role in implementing RCRA. The statute allows individual states to apply for and receive EPA's authorization to implement Subtitle C hazardous waste regulation. To be authorized, a state's program must be "equivalent to the Federal program" and "consistent with the Federal or State programs applicable in other states." RCRA §3006(b), 42 U.S.C. §6926(b). It must also provide for "adequate enforcement." *See* 40 C.F.R. §§271.1–271.27.

To date, some 48 states and the territory of Guam have received authorization to manage all or part of the RCRA Subtitle C program within their borders. States are permitted to impose requirements regarding hazardous waste that are stricter than what federal law would mandate. However, the statute preempts any state or local requirements that are less stringent than

EPA's federal requirements. RCRA § 3009, 42 U.S.C. § 6929. *See also* 40 C.F.R. § 271.1(i).

Notwithstanding the important role of the states in regulating hazardous waste, the federal government retains important responsibilities under RCRA. Thus, even in authorized states, EPA has the authority to conduct inspections of generators, transporters, and TSDFs, and to take enforcement actions on its own against alleged violators after notice to the state. RCRA §§ 3007 and 3008(a)(2), 42 U.S.C. §§ 6927 and 6928(a)(2). And in states where no authorization has been given, EPA's federal regulations apply directly, and the Agency has full responsibility for administering the hazardous waste regulation program.

V. The Enforcement of RCRA Requirements

RCRA contemplates enforcement actions by three different types of parties: the federal government, state agencies, and individual citizens. At the federal level, EPA is authorized to take three distinct types of enforcement: administrative enforcement, and (with the cooperation and assistance of the U.S. Department of Justice) civil enforcement and criminal prosecution.

Administrative enforcement, the most commonly pursued alternative, begins with an EPA administrative order. EPA may issue such an order where it determines that a person is in violation of any RCRA regulatory requirement, or where there has been an environmental release of hazardous waste. RCRA §§ 3008(a) and 3008(h)(1), 42 U.S.C. §§ 6928(a) and 6928(h)(1). The Agency may also issue an order requiring the owner or operator of a TSDF to conduct monitoring, testing, analyses, and reporting at a facility where the presence or release of hazardous waste "may present a substantial hazard to human health." RCRA § 3013, 42 U.S.C. § 6934. Moreover, EPA is empowered to issue an order "necessary to protect public health and the environment" where it has evidence that "the past or present handling, storage, treatment, transportation or disposal of any solid or hazardous waste may present an imminent and substantial endangerment to health or the environment." RCRA § 7003, 42 U.S.C. § 6973.

The statute also allows EPA to bring a civil judicial enforcement action, for injunctive relief and/or civil penalties, in all instances in which it may issue administrative orders. Civil penalties under RCRA can be sizable. Adjusted for inflation, pursuant to the Federal Civil Penalties Inflation Act of 1990, violators of Subtitle C hazardous waste regulations may be compelled to pay up to $72,718 per day per violation. *See* RCRA § 3008(g), 42 U.S.C. § 6928(g) and 40 C.F.R. § 19.4 Table 2.

In civil judicial imminent and substantial endangerment cases, courts have broadly interpreted the phrase "may present an imminent and substantial endangerment." In defining the risk needed to support the liability standard, they have emphasized the preeminence of the word "may." Moreover, imminence has generally been read to require only that the harm poses a near-term threat, as opposed to an immediate manifestation of actual harm or damage. *See Maine People's Alliance v. Mallinckrodt, Inc.*, 471 F.3d 277 (1st Cir. 2006).

In states that have received authorization to implement the RCRA hazardous waste program, EPA's regulations require that state law provide equivalent administrative civil judicial and criminal enforcement tools. *See* 40 C.F.R. § 271.16. In addition, as noted above, so long as EPA gives the state advance notice, EPA has the power to take administrative or civil judicial enforcement actions against violators in authorized states. RCRA § 3008(a)(2), 42 U.S.C. § 6928(a)(2).

The statute authorizes private citizens to institute imminent and substantial endangerment civil actions against any person whose past or ongoing handling, storage, treatment, transportation, or disposal of solid or hazardous waste that may present an imminent hazard. RCRA § 7002(a)(1)(A), 42 U.S.C. § 6972(a)(1)(A). In addition, RCRA allows citizens to sue any person alleged to be in violation of any effective RCRA permit, standard, regulation, condition, requirement, or order. RCRA § 7002(a)(1)(A), 42 U.S.C. § 6972(a)(1)(A). Citizen plaintiffs must provide advance notice to potential defendants and regulators before they commence a citizen suit. RCRA § 7002(a)(2), 42 U.S.C. § 6972(a)(2). Citizen suits against violators may not be instituted where EPA or a state "has commenced and is diligently prosecuting a civil or criminal action in a court of the United States or a State to require compliance." RCRA § 7002(b)(1)(B), 42 U.S.C. § 6972(b)(1)(B).

Checkpoints

- Subtitle D of RCRA bans "open dumps" and requires that non-hazardous solid waste be deposited in "sanitary landfills," consistent with EPA-established criteria.
- The collection and disposal of solid waste is meant to take place at the state and local level, with guidance and assistance from EPA.
- Subtitle C of RCRA is intended to protect human health and the environment from the risks created by hazardous waste.
- The statutory definition of "hazardous waste" requires that, to be considered hazardous, a waste must first satisfy the statute's definition of a "solid waste." EPA interprets "solid waste" broadly to include materials that are semi-solid, liquid, contained gases, or improperly recycled.
- EPA's subtitle C regulations identify two types of hazardous waste: characteristic hazardous waste (which has one or more hazardous characteristics) and listed hazardous waste (which EPA has specifically identified as hazardous).
- EPA established regulations for hazardous waste characteristics that can be detected by using a standard test method: ignitability, reactivity, corrosiveness, and toxicity.
- Seventeen specific waste types (including household wastes and many mining wastes) have been excluded by Congress and/or EPA from RCRA Subtitle C regulation.
- EPA's RCRA regulations contain specific requirements that apply to generators and transporters of hazardous waste and to owners and operators of treatment, storage, and disposal facilities (TSDFs).
- The statute and EPA's regulations discourage the land disposal of hazardous waste, require "corrective action" where hazardous chemicals escape from TSDFs, and impose technical and financial assurance requirements on regulated facilities.
- Under RCRA, persons who own, operate, or plan to construct a new TSDF must obtain a permit to do so.
- Facilities in existence prior to the enactment of RCRA were allowed to continue to operate temporarily, in an "interim status," so long as they complied with interim status standards and filed a permit application.
- EPA's regulations impose numerous, strict requirements on owners and operators of TSDFs with regard to such matters as hazardous waste sampling and monitoring, recordkeeping, employee training, preventing and responding to emergency events, and closure and post-closure procedures.
- Individual states may be authorized to administer hazardous waste programs that are "equivalent" to the federal program, consistent with other states' programs, and have adequate provisions for enforcement.

- RCRA contemplates enforcement action by three types of actors: the federal government, states, and private citizens.
- EPA is authorized to take three distinct types of enforcement actions: administrative and (through the Department of Justice) civil judicial, and criminal.
- States that have been authorized to implement an RCRA hazardous waste management program must have enacted state laws that provide enforcement tools equivalent to those available to EPA.
- Private citizens may (after giving prior written notice) commence civil judicial actions against violators of RCRA requirements. However, such suits are barred where EPA or a state is "diligently prosecuting" a civil or criminal action to require compliance.

Chapter 7

The Toxic Substances Control Act (TSCA) and the Federal Insecticide, Fungicide, and Rodenticide Act (FIFRA)

Roadmap

- Navigate the reporting and disclosure frameworks for persons who handle chemicals in commerce that fall under TSCA.
- Learn how persons who want to manufacture or import new chemicals must notify the U.S. Environmental Protection Agency (EPA) and, sometimes, test those chemicals.
- Find out how persons who want to use existing chemicals in new ways must alert EPA and meet possible limits on how they change those uses.
- Grasp how persons who discover new information about hazards posed by chemicals that they handle must report that information to EPA.
- Understand how TSCA sets out special requirements for certain chemicals, including asbestos, lead, and polychlorinated biphenyls (PCBs).
- Explore how EPA regulates insecticides and other poisons under an entirely different law that requires manufacturers to share their information about the chemicals and requires users of those chemicals to comply with instructions set out in mandatory labels.
- Learn how Congress recently revamped the chemicals testing and notification requirements in TSCA, and how those reforms will affect future chemicals management.

During the burst of legislative activity that created modern U.S. environmental law in the early 1970s, one of the earliest landmarks was the Toxic Substances Control Act of 1976 (TSCA). This landmark statute has served as stable bedrock for industrial chemicals management in the United States, and Congress amended it in relatively minor ways during the next 40 years.

This stability provided a constant framework for the distribution and use of chemicals. It masked, however, a growing concern that the statute's fundamental approach—to register and disclose key information about chemicals prior to their distribution in commerce—had failed to produce timely and effective management of a vast and fast-growing universe of complex chemicals without full comprehension of their toxicological or ecological risks.

To answer these concerns, Congress enacted the Frank R. Lautenberg Chemical Safety for the 21st Century Act ("Lautenberg Act") in 2016. The Lautenberg Act revamps EPA's use of the master chemical inventory and how EPA prioritizes its review and evaluation of listed chemicals. The Act also adds important new definitions, expands EPA's testing authority, narrows confidential business information exemptions, and modifies the ways that TSCA can preempt state laws that regulate chemicals. Given several statutory deadlines in the Lautenberg Act and the need to clarify sweeping new program requirements, TSCA has become one of the most active areas of environmental law and regulations.

By contrast, while TSCA focuses on the toxicological dimensions of all chemicals sold in commerce in the United States, an entirely different federal statute controls the sale and use of chemicals that are intentionally harmful or dangerous—i.e., pesticides and insecticides. Under the Federal Insecticide, Fungicide, and Rodenticide Act (FIFRA), EPA requires manufacturers and distributors of these chemicals to register them, provide important information on their safety and effectiveness, and supply mandatory labels that tell how to safely handle and use the chemicals.

This chapter describes the most important provisions of each statute and the regulatory programs that implement them. It includes an examination of the recent major revisions to TSCA. It will also examine the process that each chemical must travel to gain approval for marketing and distribution in the modern economy: registration, testing (if required), notification for changes in use, alerts for any new information about the risks or releases posed by the chemical, special cases for certain dangerous chemicals, and binding obligations on persons who handle pesticides to comply with directions on their proper use. This chapter also explores how federal regulations and decisions under TSCA and FIFRA can bind, or preempt, states that want to impose different state legal requirements for these chemicals.

It bears mention that TSCA also authorizes the regulation of nanoscale materials, polychlorinated biphenyls, asbestos and genetically modified organisms. Because of the unique regulatory status of those materials, however, regulation of them under TSCA is beyond the scope of this chapter.

I. TSCA—The Basic Framework

Most federal environmental statutes begin at the end: they only exercise jurisdiction over the wastes or pollutants that result from industrial processes, but they don't seek to control or modify the manufacturing process that created them. *See, e.g., American Mining Congress v. EPA,* 824 F.2d 1177 (D.C. Cir. 1987) (RCRA only gives EPA the power to regulate materials after they have been "discarded"). By contrast, TSCA and FIFRA focus on the manufacturing process itself. Those statutes require manufacturers or importers to notify EPA of their plans to create the substances, register them, include relevant information (if requested) about their risks, report and keep records about the substances, and follow EPA's directions on whether to limit or prohibit the manufacture of the chemicals. EPA policies therefore form a key part of private sector decisions as to whether or not to produce and distribute chemicals as a manufacturing activity.

TSCA provides EPA with several important tools to govern the processes that create chemicals in the United States. These tools include:

- Authority to Require Notification Prior to Manufacturing.
- Power to Mandate Testing of Chemicals.
- Ability to Prohibit or Limit Production and Management of Existing Chemicals.
- Certification and Notification Requirements for Imports and Exports.
- Recordkeeping and Reporting Requirements.

In addition to these powers under TSCA, EPA is authorized to oversee the production and use of pesticides under FIFRA. In particular, FIFRA gives EPA the ability to require the reporting of data to prove the effectiveness and safety of pesticides prior to their use, and to mandate that labels on pesticides provide adequate instructions on how to use and dispose of the chemicals in a safe fashion. These labels have bite. Users are required by federal law to use registered pesticides only according to the directions set out in their labels.

EPA has had these basic authorities under TSCA and FIFRA since the creation of the statutes in the 1970s. The recent passage of the Lautenberg Act did not take away powers from EPA, but it did impose mandatory deadlines for EPA to complete a revamping of its master inventory of chemicals, revise its processes for evaluating those chemicals' risks, and reprioritize which chemicals get attention first from the registration and testing process. The Act also expands and modifies the ways that TSCA preempts state chemical laws and regulations. At this writing, EPA is in the process of finalizing the regulations that will implement these changes under the Lautenberg Act. Nonetheless, this chapter will provide an overview of how that Act made important alterations to the TSCA program and shaped new legal strategies for making and managing commercial chemicals in the United States.

A. Stepping into TSCA's Jurisdiction

Before the requirements of TSCA can apply to the management of a chemical, the person handling the chemical must first undertake an action that triggers the statute's regulatory reach. In particular, TSCA applies to persons or companies that manufacture, process, distribute, use, or dispose of regulated chemicals. The statute, however, does not provide a definition for "use" or "dispose," and its definitions of "manufacture," "distribute," and "process" offer few details that help identify what activities fall within them. To compound the confusion, EPA has promulgated regulations for these terms that vary from the statute and limit their scope in important ways. As a result, persons wanting to know if TSCA applies to their activities may find themselves struggling in murky legal terrain.

A few key signposts can help, however. First, EPA's regulatory definition of "manufacture"—a major gateway for TSCA jurisdiction—adds important new elements to the statutory definition. It includes the importation of TSCA-regulated chemicals, for example, within the definition of "manufacture," and the regulatory definition limits the term to persons who manufacture chemicals "for commercial purposes." These purposes include manufacturing chemicals for "obtaining an immediate or eventual commercial advantage for the manufacturer," and they can include distribution for commerce (including test marketing) and use by the manufacturer (including product research and development). 40 C.F.R. §§ 717.3(e), 712.3(h), 704.3, 716.3, and 720.3(r). EPA's regulations also define "manufacture" to include extracting a chemical from another chemical or mixture, and they extend the term to encompass all manufacturers in certain circumstances. 40 C.F.R. § 704.3, 716.3, and 720.3(t).

The statutory definition of "process" also casts a broad net. The term includes the preparation of a chemical substance or mixture, after its manufacture, for distribution in commerce (including in articles that contain the chemical substance). TSCA § 3(13). Potentially, this definition could subject to TSCA regulation literally thousands of persons and corporations that Congress likely never meant to include within TSCA, and EPA had promulgated rules that limited TSCA's reporting requirements to only some processors. Subsequent attempts to clarify the definition further stalled after EPA invited comments from the manufacturing community, however. Those proposed clarifications have remained dormant at EPA since 1992.

The statutory terms "distribution in commerce," "use," and "disposal" either have broad definitions under TSCA or remain entirely undefined by the statute. EPA has not promulgated comprehensive guidance or regulations to clarify or narrow these terms. Nonetheless, TSCA's broad and vague statutory definitions give EPA considerable leeway to assert jurisdiction over chemical management activities if and when it so chooses.

The 2016 amendments to TSCA did not substantially change these bedrock statutory definitions. They instead added several key new terms. For example, as discussed below, the revised TSCA now includes a definition for "conditions of use" that helps focus the reviews that EPA must conduct on new and existing chemicals. The amendments also included a new definition for "potentially exposed or susceptible subpopulation," which effectively requires EPA to consider the special risks posed to these groups of people when it weighs whether a chemical poses an unreasonable risk and needs control. TSCA §§ 3(4), (12).

B. The Master Chemical Inventory

The engine for TSCA's regulation of chemicals lies in its requirement that EPA compile and maintain a list of all chemicals manufactured or processed for commercial purposes in the United States. This Master Chemical Inventory essentially dictates whether a chemical is "existing" (because the Inventory already contains it) or "new." This distinction plays an important regulatory role because TSCA imposes different notification, registration, and testing requirements for "new" chemicals than the mandates that the statute applies to "existing" chemicals.

EPA's original reporting regulations in 1977 required the addition of a chemical if it qualified as a "reportable chemical substance." To do so, the chemical had to meet three requirements: (i) it was a "chemical substance"; (ii) it was manufactured, imported, or processed for a commercial purpose in the United States between January 1, 1975 and June 1, 1979 (the date when EPA first published the Master Inventory); and (iii) the chemical was not specifically excluded from the Inventory.

The first requirement—classification as a "chemical substance"—was straightforward because the regulation essentially incorporated the statutory definition of "chemical substance" to include any organic or inorganic substance of a "particular molecular identity." These chemicals could include any combination of substances that occurred in whole or in part as a chemical reaction or that occurred in nature. These conditions were limited, however, by statutory exclusions for any mixture, any commercial pesticide, tobacco and certain tobacco products, nuclear source materials or by-products, firearms and ammunition, and any commercial food, food additive, drug, cosmetic, or device.

By contrast, the other two requirements for "reportable chemical substances" are relatively straightforward. The mandate that the chemical be manufactured or imported for "a commercial purpose" only requires that a given chemical be manufactured or imported for distribution in commerce (including test marketing) or for use by the manufacturer or importer (including as an intermediate). Specific exclusions remove the need to list chemical substances used only in small quantities for research and development, pesticides, articles (i.e., manufactured items formed into a specific shape or design that don't undergo a change of chemical composition during its use), impurities, by-products, chemicals produced by incidental reactions, or non-isolated chemical intermediates.

Searching the Master Chemical Inventory is usually a simple task where a manufacturer or importer has a chemical's CAS registry number or other index. Some chemicals, however, may be listed in versions designated as confidential by their manufacturer or importer. To search confidential portions of the Inventory, a party will need to demonstrate that it has a *bona fide* intent to manufacture or import the chemical substance for a commercial purpose. To do so, a party will need to submit a notice of *bona fide* intent to manufacture or import the chemical, which will require it to give EPA basic information about the chemical and its plans to handle it, along with fundamental analytical information about the chemical (such as an elemental analysis and spectrographic information).

Once a manufacturer or importer of a particular chemical locates it on the TSCA Inventory, they many start immediately to manufacture or import the chemical. If the Inventory doesn't include the chemical, however—and if the chemical doesn't qualify for one of the exemptions from the listing requirement—the manufacturer or importer must proceed to consider it a new chemical under TSCA.

C. New Chemicals—Notifications

New chemicals not on the TSCA Inventory face an entirely different regulatory gauntlet. First, anyone who wants to manufacture or import a new unlisted chemical must provide EPA with a premanufacture notice (PMN). This PMN must include information about basic parameters of the chemical, including its identity, use, how much would be produced, any test data about the chemical's effects on health or the environment, and a description of other data about health or environmental effects that the submitter knows or can "reasonably ascertain."

The PMN serves a critical gateway function for regulation of new chemicals under TSCA. In essence, the PMN allows EPA to hold manufacturers and importers responsible for developing adequate data about the chemical's effects on health and the environment. This policy, however, does not require the submitter to perform any specific tests as part of the PMN (unless the chemical is subject to a testing rule under TSCA section 4, which we'll discuss shortly). As a result, TSCA in its classic form—before Congress amended the statute in 2016—did not compel submitters to prepare a set of basic premarket data for new chemicals. EPA, however, can now prohibit or limit the manufacturing, processing, distribution, or use of the chemical, where the Agency determines that it lacks sufficient information for a reasoned evaluation of the chemical's effects and the chemical may either present an unreasonable risk or result in significant human exposure. TSCA § 5(a)(3)(A).

Once EPA receives a PMN application for a significant new use of an existing chemical (discussed below), the 2016 revisions to TSCA require EPA to determine whether the chemical "presents or will present an unreasonable risk of injury to health or the environment." TSCA §§ 6(a), (b)(1)(B)(i). In making that decision, EPA must satisfy several statutory requirements. Specifically, the Agency must decide: (i) whether the chemical presents an unreasonable risk of injury to health or the environment, (ii) whether EPA lacks sufficient information to make a reasoned evaluation of the chemical, and (iii) whether or not the chemical may present an unreasonable risk, and (if it does) whether the product will be produced in sufficiently substantial quantities that it will be problematic. If EPA finds that the chemical does not pose an unreasonable risk, the submitter may proceed to manufacture or process the chemical immediately. Otherwise, EPA must issue an order under TSCA Section 5(e) or promulgate a significant new use rule for the chemical.

To weigh the risk posed by a chemical, EPA must take several steps within tight statutory deadlines. First, it must decide whether the chemical is to be afforded high priority because it may present an unreasonable risk because of a potential hazard and a potential route of exposure. In fact, EPA must conduct risk evaluations on all high-priority chemicals, and it must complete its evaluation within one year. If the Agency fails to meet the one-year deadline, the chemical is to be considered a high-priority item by default.

Second, EPA must perform a risk evaluation of all high-priority chemicals to see whether they pose an unreasonable risk to susceptible subpopulations.

EPA must complete its high-priority risk evaluations within three and one-half years; and in conducting those evaluations the Agency may not consider costs or other non-risk factors. Finally, the TSCA amendments require EPA to propose a within one year, and finalize within another year, a rule that chooses a protective risk management option. At this final stage, EPA may consider costs, benefits, economic consequences, and the availability of safer alternatives. TSCA § 6.

As with existing chemicals, the PMN requirements do not apply to materials excluded from the definition of "chemical substance," such as mixtures, pesticides, foods, drugs, cosmetics, nuclear materials, and tobacco products. In addition, TSCA adds two other exemptions specifically to the PMN program: test marketing, and research and development. Under TSCA § 5(h)(1), new chemical substances manufactured for test marketing purposes do not require a PMN if the EPA Administrator concludes that the test marketing activities will not pose an unreasonable risk to human health or the environment. The test marketer must apply for the exemption and demonstrate that the test marketing won't pose an unreasonable risk. By contrast, TSCA exempts small amounts of new chemicals from PMN requirements if they are used solely for research and development under supervision by a qualified individual (so long as the manufacturer alerts the researchers about any health risks posed by the chemical). Unlike the test marketing exemption, the research and development exclusion does not require prior agency approval. 40 C.F.R. § 720.36.

In addition to test marketing and research and development, TSCA includes numerous other narrow exemptions from PMN requirements for certain niche chemicals or certain low-volume uses. For example, TSCA wholly excludes certain types of polymers, chemicals imported in articles, chemicals formed during the manufacture of an article, and chemicals formed incidentally during the use of certain additives. EPA has clarified that this "additives exemption" only applies to substances formed from chemical reactions during the use of the chemical, the substance doesn't provide one or more primary properties of the ultimate product, and the substance itself isn't intended for distribution in commerce.

D. Existing Chemicals — Significant New Uses

Sometimes, rather than create an entirely new chemical, a user may wish to put an existing chemical to a new use. Given the large number of chemicals already included on the Master Inventory, the regulation of "significant new uses" necessarily plays a central role in TSCA oversight.

Where a party proposes to deploy a chemical already on the Inventory in a way that EPA considers a "significant new use," that party must first provide EPA with a Significant New Use Notice (SNUN). In response, the agency may choose to issue a Significant New Use Rule (SNUR). After EPA issues the SNUR on an existing chemical, any person who wants to manufacture or process that substance must give 90 calendar days prior notice to EPA. Once a submitter provides its notification, the proposed new use of the existing chemical undergoes the same risk evaluation for new chemicals described earlier.

To fully implement TSCA's regulation of new uses for existing chemicals, EPA has developed several regulatory tools to provide more flexibility. For example, the Generic SNUR Rule streamlines and standardizes the processes EPA uses to regulate standardized new uses, recordkeeping requirements, and notice-and-comment protocols for rulemaking. The Generic SNUR Rule sets out give broad categories of chemical uses that fall within its purview. Each category shares a few fundamental characteristics: the commercial activity involves a risk for which a protective standard does not yet exist, deals with a release or disposal of particular listed hazardous substances, and falls within a broad "catchall" section that gives EPA broad authority to regulate the chemical's management. In addition, the Generic SNUR Rule gives EPA the power to use expedited procedures to impose SNURs on chemicals that are already the subject of TSCA § 5(e) orders.

E. Testing and Testing Orders

When the risks of new or existing chemicals remain unknown, TSCA gives EPA the authority to compel manufacturers and processors to create data on the environmental and health effects of their chemicals. This power arises in two circumstances: when a chemical is produced in substantial quantities and may result in substantial human or environmental exposure ("exposure based"), or when the chemical itself may pose an unreasonable risk of injury ("risk-based"). For risk-based test rules, EPA may require testing if: (i) it finds that the chemical (or a mixture containing it) may present an unreasonable risk of injury to human health or the environment, (ii) the existing data on that chemical won't suffice to allow reasonable predictions or determinations of its effects, and (iii) testing is necessary to develop those data. EPA may only require testing if some possibility of exposure exists. TSCA, however, allows EPA to rely on inferences to establish "a more-than-theoretical probability of exposure." *Chemical Manufacturers Ass'n. v. EPA*, 859 F.2d 977, 989 (D.C. Cir. 1988).

By contrast, exposure-based test rules allow EPA to require testing if: (i) the chemical is produced in substantial quantities, (ii) the chemical is reasonably expected to be released into the environment in substantial quantities, (iii) insufficient data exist to allow a reasonable prediction of the chemical's effect on human health or the environment, and (iv) testing is needed to generate those data.

Consistent with decades of prior TSCA practice, EPA typically requires a testing rule for a particular chemical substance through a single-phase rulemaking. Under this procedure, EPA will specify a particular test guideline as the mandated standard for a particular chemical in an initial notice of proposed rulemaking. Although commenters (including chemical manufacturers) may suggest alternative test methods, EPA generally has discretion to specify the required test guideline in its final rule. Persons subject to a final test order must then submit a letter of intent to conduct testing or, alternatively, seek an exemption, although persons who obtain an exemption must nevertheless reimburse other persons who perform required testing for a portion of their costs. The details of this cost-sharing typically are typically determined through a voluntary agreement or, in rare cases, by arbitration. The 2016 amendments to TSCA now empower EPA to also use administrative orders and consent agreements to develop test data.

The 2016 amendments also made other important changes to EPA's authority to require testing of chemicals. In particular, TSCA Section 4(f) now has expanded EPA's authority to take expedited action if new information points to any significant risk to humans posed by a chemical. (Before the amendments, EPA could only take this action if the chemicals posed a cancer, gene mutation, or birth defect risk). Section 4(f) further requires EPA to use tiered testing (rather than jumping immediately to an advanced, more expensive, test), TSCA §4(a)(4), and the 2016 amendments direct EPA to reduce and replace vertebrate animal testing where "scientifically justified." TSCA §4(h).

F. Reporting Obligations

TSCA requires reports of information and data that EPA needs to effectively regulate unsafe chemical substances and respond to releases into the environment. Under Section 8, the statute mandates manufacturers, importers, and processors of chemicals to maintain records and submit reports to EPA about their activities. Under the authority of TSCA Section 8(a), EPA has imposed recordkeeping requirements for specific listed chemicals, and it has issued model rules for detailed manufacturing and exposure information for other listed chemicals. The Agency's most recent rule, the Inventory

Update Rule, expanded regulations that require manufacturers and importers to provide current information about production volume and exposure information for chemicals manufactured or imported in amounts above certain volume levels. That data in turn helps EPA to compile the TSCA Master Inventory described earlier.

Section 8's reporting requirements extend further. Specifically, Section 8 requires three additional categories of recordkeeping and reporting: significant adverse reactions under Section 8(c), health and safety studies under Section 8(d), and substantial risk information under Section 8(e). These reporting requirements offer a mix of recordkeeping and disclosure.

For example, Section 8(c)'s mandate that manufacturers and importers keep records of significant adverse reactions to health and the environment caused by their chemical substances or mixtures directs those parties to maintain those records for 30 years if an employee makes the allegation that he or she has suffered an adverse health effect. (If anyone else submits such an allegation, the record retention requirement shortens to five years.) Section 8(c), however, does not require the manufacturer or importer to disclose that information to EPA unless the Agency requests it.

By contrast, Section 8(d)'s Model Reporting Rule requires persons within certain categories of the North American Industry Classification System (NAICS), as well as additional persons identified by EPA in later rulemakings, to submit all non-exempt, requested studies that EPA requests when the rule first applies to them. In addition, the Model Reporting Rule orders those persons to alert EPA within 30 days of any other studies that the manufacturer or importer initiates on the chemical.

A third reporting rule, Section 8(e) substantial risk information disclosures, casts a broader net. It directs any person who manufactures, processes, imports, or distributes a chemical substance to report to EPA any information that "reasonably supports the conclusion" that the chemical "presents a substantial risk of injury to health or the environment" unless that person knows that EPA already has the information. This obligation obviously covers a broad range of information, and its blurry boundaries have historically created concerns for persons who discover new information about chemicals within their care or who suffer a spill or release of those chemicals into the environment. This statutory obligation applies, according to EPA guidance, to both senior company management and employees "who are capable of appreciating the significance of pertinent information." EPA has interpreted this statutory reporting requirement to mandate a submission of relevant information within 30 calendar days except in "emergency incidents of environmental contamination" (which require immediate reporting).

The 2016 amendments to TSCA introduced an important new element to the Section 8 notification process. Section 8(b)(4) essentially reboots the Master Inventory of existing chemicals. Under this provision, EPA has promulgated a rule requiring manufacturers to notify the Agency whether they have manufactured or processed any listed chemical during the 10-year period prior to the TSCA amendments. Based on that information, EPA will segregate the chemicals on the Master Inventory as either "active" or "inactive." TSCA § 8(b)(4).

G. Preemption and Enforcement

Many states, including (and most significantly) California and New Jersey, have their own statutes and regulations to govern management of chemicals and disclosure of information about their risks and properties. To avoid confusion and conflict, TSCA historically contained complex provisions to govern the scope and effect of its preemption of state laws, regulations, and orders (including consent decrees). In the 2016 TSCA amendments, however, Congress thoroughly revamped TSCA's preemption provisions, to expand the statute's preemptive scope.

Under the 2016 TSCA provisions, preemption can occur in four ways. Permanent preemption takes place when a state requests study data that EPA already has; when a state seeks to restrict the manufacture, processing, distribution, or use of a chemical that EPA has already concluded is safe; or where EPA has established an effective rule to regulate those risks (although states may still regulate other activities not covered in EPA's risk evaluation). States cannot demand a notification of a significant new use where EPA has already required a SNUR, but EPA can expressly waive this preemption requirement.

II. Pesticides, Insecticides, Fungicides, Rodenticides, and Other Economic Poisons within the World of FIFRA

While TSCA deals with commercial chemicals that might cause harm upon exposure, FIFRA focuses on economic poisons—chemicals designed to kill or repel animals or plant pests that can cause personal injury or financial harm. It uses a far more prescriptive regulatory approach than TSCA does, with a stronger oversight role by EPA (and, to a far lesser extent, state governments).

Like TSCA, FIFRA's regulatory scheme relies on a registration program to identify and track chemicals and substances. EPA must approve any pesticide before its manufacture, distribution, or import into the United States. Obtaining this registration is no small feat. It can require years of testing and assessment as well as millions of dollars, and the approval process at EPA can take several additional years as well. In contrast with TSCA's relatively simple registration and inventory tracking system, the FIFRA registration process is far more rigorous and challenging.

A. Gateway to FIFRA: What Is a Pesticide?

FIFRA applies to "pesticides," which it defines as any substance intended for "preventing, destroying, repelling or mitigating any pest" as well as substances meant for "use as a plant regulator, defoliant, or desiccant." Pests receive a similarly broad definition as "insects, rodents, worms, fungus, weeds, plants, virus, bacteria, microorganisms, and other animal life." And FIFRA classifies as a pesticide device an object used for "trapping, destroying, repelling or mitigating any pest or any other form of plant or animal life." Interestingly, though, FIFRA and EPA's implementing regulations exclude devices that depend on the skill of the user to kill or trap the pest—including firearms, flyswatters, traps (for vertebrate animals), and other devices.

One keystone to FIFRA's regulatory approach lies in its intent: the definition of "pesticide" turns on the intended or claimed use of the substance. As a result, a substance that lacks a claim or label calling the substance a pesticide falls outside the regulatory scope of FIFRA, even if that substance functions very effectively as a pesticide.

B. Registering Pesticides

The registration process is the heart of FIFRA's regulatory system. With only minor exceptions, all new pesticides used in the United States must first be registered with EPA. The registration application yields key information needed to weigh the pesticide's risks and proper use in commerce, including specific information about the complete formulation of the substance, its proposed label, and a compilation of the tests performed on the substance and their results. This process yields a narrow, specific registration record that focuses on the particular formulation and use of the proposed pesticide; it does not consider uses of the pesticide on other crops or pests. The registration similarly does not cover varying doses of the pesticide or differing application methods.

Once an applicant provides the required registration information, EPA must approve the application where it satisfies several conditions:

- The substance's composition warrants the proposed claim for it;
- The proposed labeling and other materials comply with FIFRA's requirements;
- The substance will achieve its desired outcome without "unreasonable adverse effects on the environment"; and
- The substance will not cause such an unreasonable adverse effect on the environment when used in accordance with widespread and commonly recognized practice.

The issue that causes the most controversy is what side effects qualify as "unreasonable adverse effects on the environment." FIFRA cryptically defines this term as "any unreasonable risk to man or the environment, taking into account the economic, social, and environmental costs and benefits of the use of the pesticide." This definition quietly packs in several important qualifications to FIFRA's protections by essentially allowing some risks—if not "unreasonable"—justified by economic or social considerations. In effect, it allows some balancing of risk, costs, and benefits, and bars FIFRA from operating as a strict liability statute.

Pesticide registrations, like loaves of bread, have a shelf life. Typically, registrations last up to 15 years without renewal. They automatically expire unless an interested party petitions for renewal of the registration and provides additional safety data if requested to do so by EPA.

Because the registration process and EPA approvals can take a long time, FIFRA provides an expedited system for conditional registration. FIFRA Section 3(c) provides for three kinds of expedited conditional registration with respect to: (i) pesticides identical or very similar to currently registered products, (ii) new uses of existing pesticide registrations, and (iii) pesticides containing active ingredients not contained in any currently registered pesticide for which data need to be obtained for registration. These conditional registrations apply on a case-by-case basis and require a finding by EPA that "use of the pesticide is in the public interest." Nonetheless, the use of conditional registration has grown over the years, and it has led to the broad use of some pesticides for many years under a "temporary" conditional authorization.

C. Efficacy, Secrecy, and Necessity

The registration process has additional goals beyond measuring the safety of proposed pesticides. In particular, EPA has the discretion to require an applicant to submit data showing that its pesticide actually works. While EPA continues to routinely request efficacy data on antimicrobials and rodenticides, it typically does not now seek efficacy data (which may affect the scope of federal preemption of state tort lawsuits over pesticide uses, as discussed below).

In addition to efficacy, the registration process also provides protection for trade secrets encompassed in registration applications. FIFRA Section 10 allows EPA to reveal trade secrets submitted with registration applications "when necessary to carry out the provisions of this Act"; in particular, the confidential data "may be revealed to any federal agency consulted and may be revealed at a public hearing or in findings of fact issued by the Administrator." Registrants must thus assume that any data they provide to EPA with their registration may, ultimately, reach the public arena where the public interest requires disclosure. In fact, however, the Agency has not frequently made such disclosures.

FIFRA's registration process does not require proof that a registered substance contains only ingredients that serve an additional useful or necessary purpose. This practice reflects two concerns. First, pesticide manufacturers grew concerned that EPA could refuse to register a new pesticide product if the market already provided an existing pesticide that satisfactorily performed in the same way. And second, manufacturers worried that EPA would point to the existence of effective existing alternatives as a factor in its willingness to cancel or suspend registrations for pesticides. While the first concern hasn't materialized in any significant way, the existence of effective alternatives can play an important role in the suspension and cancellation process (discussed below).

D. Controlling Use of Registered Pesticides

Once EPA approves the registration of a pesticide, FIFRA controls the pesticide's application through two basic tools. EPA separates pesticides into two categories—general and restricted—and requires that only certified applicators can use restricted pesticides. This approach theoretically assures that only trained and competent personnel are permitted to handle the most dangerous material. At the same time, though, FIFRA's substantive requirements regarding training are rather sparse. For example, FIFRA allows private applicators to self-certify whether they (or their employees) applied a restricted pesticide to their own property or farm after receiving special training. The statute, however, prohibits EPA from testing the applicators to assess their actual knowledge after completing the training.

Second, FIFRA Section 12 also bars the use of a pesticide in a manner inconsistent with its label or labeling. In effect, federal law requires the user to follow the instructions on the approved label. Fines for violations by private applicators, however, are typically relatively small.

Beyond actual use, FIFRA also forbids anyone from selling restricted pesticides to unauthorized applicators, altering or mutilating pesticide labels, or selling a misbranded or unregistered pesticide or making claims about the pesticide that vary from its registration or labeling.

E. Cancellations, Suspensions, and Recalls

If EPA believes that a registered pesticide now poses an unacceptable risk, FIFRA gives it two tools to take action. First, EPA is authorized to cancel the pesticide's registration. A cancellation notice essentially initiates a review of a substance suspected of posing a "substantial question of safety" to humans and the environment. This cancellation notice can take several forms, including cancellations where the substance presents a highly probable threat to man or the environment but there is not sufficient evidence or urgency to warrant an immediate suspension. Less urgently, cancellations can also arise when scientific tests identify some cause for concern that justifies a public hearing or scientific advisory committee inquiry. And last, cancellations can result from citizen suits as a tool to allow the marshaling and presentation of information about the disputed chemical.

Cancellation, despite its implied undertone of urgency, is a cumbersome process. A cancellation order (unless undisputed) usually requires a public hearing and/or a scientific review committee assessment, and review steps can include presentation to an administrative law judge and judicial review. As a result, a contested cancellation order can easily take years to complete and implement.

By contrast, a suspension order imposes an immediate ban on the production and distribution of a registered pesticide. FIFRA mandates the issuance of a suspension order when a pesticide poses an imminent hazard to human health or the environment, and EPA can impose a suspension order at any time during the lengthy cancellation process (or even before a cancellation effort begins).

Suspensions come in two flavors. Ordinary suspensions typically mitigate an imminent hazard while a cancellation proceeding is underway. In effect, they operate as FIFRA's equivalent to a preliminary injunction to provide temporary, limited relief while the full proceeding moves ahead. Unless a registrant requests an expedited hearing within five days of the order's issuance, it takes effect immediately. Typically, a court cannot review a suspension order.

Emergency suspensions operate differently. They immediately halt all uses, sales, and distributions of the pesticide. EPA may issue an emergency suspension *ex parte* without an opportunity for notice and hearing before the order takes effect. To use this authority, however, EPA must first determine that an emergency exists that prevents the agency from holding a hearing before the pesticide's suspension. While rarely invoked, emergency suspension orders are one of the most powerful actions that EPA can take under FIFRA.

In addition to cancellations and suspensions, EPA may also order the recall of misbranded pesticides already in commerce. Typically, EPA has allowed owners of banned pesticides to use their existing stocks after EPA has issued a cancellation or suspension order. This strategy typically reflects EPA's exercise of enforcement discretion in light of administrative and practical concerns, including fears that collection and disposal of banned pesticides may actually result in concentrations more harmful to the environment than dispersal of the remaining stocks. 56 Fed. Reg. 29362 (June 26, 1991). Although environmental groups have repeatedly challenged this tactic, the courts have typically rejected these challenges. *See, e.g., National Coalition Against the Misuse of Pesticides v. EPA*, 867 F.2d 636 (D.C. Cir. 1989); *Environmental Defense Fund v. EPA*, 510 F.2d 1292 (D.C. Cir. 1975).

F. A Final Word: Preemption of State Law and Tort Liability

Given the natural tension between state and local governments who want more stringent management requirements for pesticides used in their jurisdictions and pesticide manufacturers and distributors who fear a tangle of conflicting local requirements, FIFRA provides some guidance on how EPA's federal actions preempt state regulatory efforts. Unfortunately, that guidance is ambiguous.

FIFRA Section 24(b) provides that a state "shall not impose or continue in effect any requirements for labeling or packaging in addition to or different from those required under [FIFRA]." Section 24 also assures states, however, that they can "regulate the sale or use of any pesticide or device in the state, but only if and to the extent that the regulation does not permit any sale or use prohibited by [FIFRA.]" This congressional elision has naturally resulted in a welter of conflicting judicial decisions attempting to gauge the scope of FIFRA's preemptive effect on state pesticide regulations and local use requirements.

In general, the courts have struck the following balance. States and localities may implement their own requirements governing the use of a pesticide where those requirements do not conflict with FIFRA-regulated label claims. This zone of flexibility has allowed cities to govern some of the mechanics of pesticide product application, including requiring warning signs and/or local permits for spraying public lands. Other states, notably California, have implemented their own state-law based chemical registration and informational tracking systems.

FIFRA's preemptive effect on state tort liability claims arising from pesticide use, however, has proven more problematic. After the U.S. Supreme Court resolved similar preemption issues in its *Cipollone v. Liggett Group* decision, 505 U.S. 504 (1992), regarding whether and how federal labeling requirements preempted state law tort actions for damages from cigarette consumption, a welter of subsequent federal court decisions have found that FIFRA can preempt state tort actions. The precise scope of the preemption depends heavily on the specific actions underlying the tort and the type of tort action alleged. *See, e.g., Bates v. Dow Agrosciences LLC,* 544 U.S. 431 (2005) (state tort claims for defective labeling preempted, but not defective manufacture or design); *Indian Brand Farms, Inc. v. Novartis Crop Protection, Inc.,* 617 F.3d 207 (3d Cir. 2010); *Wuebker v. Wilber Ellis Co.,* 418 F.3d 883 (8th Cir. 2005); *Peterson v. BASF Corp.,* 711 N.W.2d 470 (Minn. 2006). The pertinent decisions roughly hold that federal preemption does bar tort actions over the adequacy of pesticide labels that EPA had previously approved, but it does not limit suits alleging product defects, faulty tests, or warranty claims.

Checkpoints

- TSCA gives EPA the authority to regulate certain activities regarding the production and distribution of chemicals, including:
  - Manufacturing, but typically only for a commercial purpose.
  - Processing, which can include any person who prepares a chemical substance or mixture *after* its manufacture, but again only for distribution in commerce (i.e., for a commercial purpose).
  - "Using" the chemical in a manufacturing process, which TSCA does not define, and EPA has not promulgated a regulatory definition to narrow the term.
  - Importation of chemicals, which is classified as manufacturing.
- TSCA requires EPA to maintain a master inventory of all chemicals used in commerce. To add or modify a chemical's inventory listing, TSCA requires manufacturers or importers to obtain either a Premanufacturing Notice (for new chemicals) or a Significant New Use Registration (for existing chemicals). At either of these registration steps EPA can require an applicant to provide data or testing to EPA upon the Agency's request.
- EPA can require manufacturers and importers to test their chemicals and submit data under testing orders. In addition, they may also have an obligation under TSCA to report data or information about significant risks or adverse effects.
- FIFRA requires manufacturers to register their pesticides with EPA and obtain labels that prescribe the correct ways to use them.
  - Applicants must submit comprehensive test and safety data on the exact formulation of the pesticide and exactly how it will be used. Future labels will approve only the uses set out in the data, and other uses or formulations are not approved.
  - Parties may only use pesticides according to the instructions and warnings on their EPA-approved labels. Failure to do so violates FIFRA and can trigger both civil and criminal liability.
  - Only certified applicators can buy and use substances that EPA has classified as "restricted pesticides."
  - EPA is authorized to cancel or suspend a registration if the substance poses either an unwarranted risk (for cancellations) or an imminent hazard (for suspensions) to human health or the environment.
  - EPA regulatory requirements and approved labeling can preempt conflicting state law requirements, but states may still impose some place and use restrictions on where and how pesticides are used. EPA-approved labels may preempt some state law tort claims as well, but that preemption by label does not extend to other facets of the pesticide, such as product defects or substandard testing.

Chapter 8

The National Environmental Policy Act

Roadmap

- Learn the most critical provisions of the National Environmental Policy Act (NEPA).
- Understand how NEPA has been enforced in the federal courts.
- Grasp what an environmental impact statement (EIS) is and under what circumstances it must be prepared.
- Comprehend what is meant by the statutory phrase "major federal action."
- Understand how the Council on Environmental Quality (CEQ) and the federal courts have interpreted "significantly affecting the quality of the human environment" for purposes of NEPA.
- Learn the procedures agencies must follow in deciding whether to prepare an EIS, and in actually preparing such a document.
- Comprehend how federal courts review the adequacy of an EIS.
- Grasp the potential significance of NEPA's "Interpretation Mandate."
- Understand the remedies commonly awarded to successful plaintiffs in NEPA litigation.

I. Introduction and Overview

The National Environmental Policy Act ("NEPA"), 42 U.S.C. § 4321 et seq., was the first piece of environmental legislation enacted in the modern era of environmental law. Passed amidst a loud and broad public outcry for a governmental response to a host of serious national environmental problems, the Act includes both lofty statements of purposes and policies and certain specific action-forcing provisions that apply to all federal agencies and departments. It also creates a new entity within the Executive Branch, the Council on Environmental Quality (CEQ), to study and report on environmental trends and advise the president on environmental issues.

This chapter first considers the key provisions of NEPA, how the statute can be enforced, and how the federal courts have determined whether the statute imposes substantive (rather than procedural) duties to protect the environment. It then focuses on a critical action-forcing mandate of NEPA: the requirement that responsible federal officials prepare an environmental impact statement ("EIS") for every major federal action that significantly affects the quality of the human environment. This chapter explores the circumstances that trigger the requirement to prepare an EIS, and what an EIS must contain to meet NEPA's requirements. Finally, it examines the remedies that courts have imposed on federal agencies to redress NEPA violations.

II. The Nature of NEPA

A. Critical Statutory Provisions

NEPA begins with a grandiloquent statement of purpose and a bold and far-reaching national policy. It states that the purposes of the Act are "to declare a national policy which will encourage productive and enjoyable harmony between man and his environment; to promote efforts which will prevent or eliminate damage to the environment and biosphere and stimulate the health and welfare of man; to enrich the understanding of the ecological systems and natural resources important to the Nation; and to Establish a Council on Environmental Quality." NEPA § 2, 42 U.S.C. § 4321. The statute goes on to declare that "it is the continuing policy of the Federal Government, in cooperation with State and local governments, and other concerned public and private organizations, to use all practicable means and measures, including financial and technical assistance, in a manner calculated to foster and promote the general welfare, to create and maintain conditions under which man and nature can exist in productive harmony, and fulfill the social, economic, and other requirements of present and future generations of Americans." NEPA § 101(a), 42 U.S.C. § 4331(a).

To implement these purposes and policies, the Act contains some specific provisions that apply to all agencies of the federal government "to the fullest extent possible." First, NEPA contains an interpretation mandate. It directs that "the policies, regulations, and public laws of the United States shall be interpreted and administered in accordance with the policies set forth in this Act." NEPA § 102(1), 42 U.S.C. § 4332(1). Second, in planning and decision-making that may impact the environment, federal agencies must "utilize a systematic, interdisciplinary approach which will ensure the integrated use of the natural and social sciences and the environmental design arts . . ." NEPA § 102(2)(A), 42 U.S.C. § 4332(2)(A). Third, all federal agencies must "identify and develop measures and procedures . . . which will ensure that presently unquantified environmental amenities and values may be given appropriate consideration in decision-making, along with economic and technical considerations." NEPA § 102(2)(B), 42 U.S.C. § 4332(2)(B).

All federal agencies are also required to initiate and utilize ecological information in the planning and development of resource-oriented projects. NEPA § 102(2)(H), 42 U.S.C. § 4332(2)(H). They must "study, develop, and describe appropriate alternatives to recommended courses of action in any proposal which involves unresolved alternative uses of available resources." NEPA § 102(2)(E), 42 U.S.C. § 4332(2)(E). And they are directed to recognize the worldwide and long-range character of environmental problems, and "lend appropriate support to initiatives, resolutions, and programs" that will "maximize international cooperation in anticipating and preventing a decline in the quality of mankind's world environment." NEPA § 102(2)(F), 42 U.S.C. § 4332(2)(F).

The action-forcing provision of NEPA that has drawn the most attention, however, is the statute's environmental impact statement requirement. NEPA mandates that all federal agencies include "in every recommendation or report on proposals for legislation," and other "major Federal actions significantly affecting the quality of the human environment," a detailed statement by the responsible official. This statement, commonly referred to as an EIS, must set forth five items: (i) the environmental impact of the proposed action, (ii) any adverse environmental effects that cannot be avoided should the proposal be implemented, (iii) alternatives to the proposed action, (iv) the relationship between local short-term uses of the environment and the maintenance and enhancement of long-term productivity, and (v) any irreversible and irretrievable commitments of resources that would be involved in the proposed action should it be implemented. NEPA § 102(2)(C), 42 U.S.C. § 4332(2)(C).

B. The Enforceability of NEPA

Initially, many federal agencies were resistant to implementing their new obligations under NEPA in a prompt and full fashion. An early example of this attitude was the Atomic Energy Commission ("the AEC") (now the Nuclear Regulatory Commission), which was at first quite reluctant to allow the consideration of environmental impacts to impede the development of a nuclear power industry in the United States. The AEC's approach to NEPA implementation was challenged in an important case decided by the U.S. Court of Appeals for the D.C. Circuit, *Calvert Cliffs' Coordinating Committee, Inc. v. U.S. Atomic Energy Commission,* 449 F.2d 1109 (D.C. Cir. 1971). In that case, the court established several principles that proved influential and subsequent judicial interpretations. It ruled that NEPA makes environmental protection "a part of the mandate of every federal agency and department," and noted that the Act contains "very important 'procedural' provisions" that are "not highly flexible," and that "establish a strict standard of compliance." *Id.*

The D.C. Circuit also considered the purpose of an EIS. It concluded that that purpose was "to aid in the agency's own decision-making process, and to advise other interested agencies and the public of the environmental consequences of planned federal action." *Id.* According to the court, NEPA mandates a "careful and informed decision-making process" within federal agencies, and it creates "judicially enforceable duties." *Id.* Environmental factors compiled in an EIS must thus be considered through agency review processes "at every important stage in the decision-making process—at every stage where an overall balancing of environmental and non-environmental factors is appropriate and where alterations might be made in the proposed action to minimize environmental costs." This internal agency consideration process is intended to create a case-by-case balancing analysis, in which the economic and technical benefits of planned actions are to be assessed and weighed against environmental costs and possible alternatives, with the goal of ensuring that "the optimally beneficial action" is finally taken. *Id.*

Subsequent judicial interpretations of NEPA emphasized that although the statute does not expressly create a right of action, citizens concerned that a federal agency has not complied with a NEPA requirement may seek relief under the judicial review provisions of the Administrative Procedure Act, 5 U.S.C. §§ 701 to 706. These provisions allow courts only to review "final agency actions." Thus, citizen plaintiffs are required to wait until an agency has taken action before they may initiate litigation alleging that the agency has violated NEPA. *See, e.g., Public Citizen v. U.S. Trade Representative*, 5 F.3d 549 (D.C. Cir. 1993).

C. Substance versus Procedure in NEPA Compliance

Important as it was as a precedent that established a strict procedural requirement for federal agencies, the *Calvert Cliffs* decision did not conclusively decide another important question that arose in subsequent NEPA lawsuits: did the statute require particular substantive results after an agency has prepared an EIS? In the 1980s, the U.S. Supreme Court handed down a series of opinions that resolved that issue in the negative.

In *Strykers Bay Neighborhood Council, Inc. v. Karlen*, 444 U.S. 223 (1980), the Court considered a NEPA challenge to a decision by the U.S. Department of Housing and Urban Development ("HUD") to approve a local plan to construct a high-rise apartment building, consisting entirely of low-income housing, at a site on the west side of Manhattan. The Supreme Court reversed a decision of the United States Court of Appeals for the Second Circuit that had set aside HUD's decision to fund the building in question for failing to give environmental considerations "determinative weight." Instead, the Court held that "once an agency has made a decision subject to NEPA's procedural requirements, the only role for a court is to ensure that the agency has considered the environmental consequences; it cannot interject itself within the area of discretion of the executives as to the choice of the action to be taken." *Id.*

This conclusion was reiterated by the Supreme Court, in a *per curiam* opinion in *Robertson v. Methow Valley Citizens Council*, 490 U.S. 332 (1989), a citizens' challenge to an EIS prepared by the U.S. Forest Service. The EIS in issue noted that significant environmental harm would result from the construction of a ski resort within a national forest, in the event that it was permitted by the Forest Service and constructed, but the statement failed to require any specific steps to mitigate that harm. Citing *Stryker's Bay*, the Court stated that "an EIS merely prohibits uninformed—rather than unwise—agency action." *Id.* The Court reasoned that "it would be inconsistent with NEPA's reliance on procedural mechanisms—as opposed to substantive, results-based standards—to demand the presence of a fully developed plan that will mitigate environmental harm before an agency can act." *Id.* It concluded that "if the adverse environmental effects of the proposed action are adequately identified and evaluated, the agency is not constrained by NEPA from deciding that other values outweigh the environmental costs." *Id.*

III. Triggering the Requirement to Prepare an EIS

As noted previously, NEPA commands federal agencies to include "in every recommendation or report on proposals for legislation and other major federal actions significantly affecting the quality of the human environment" a detailed statement on, among other things, the environment impact of the proposed action. NEPA § 102(2)(c), 42 U.S.C. § 4332(2)(c). The "trigger" that requires preparation of an EIS has several components. First, it must be determined whether what an agency has in mind is a "proposal." If so the agency's proposal must be for a "major federal action." And third, assuming those two conditions are satisfied, the agency's proposal must "significantly affect the quality of the human environment."

A. What Is a Proposal?

In 1978, the Council on Environment Quality published regulations that define much of the nomenclature of NEPA and guide federal agencies in its implementation. *See* 40 C.F.R. pt. 1502. These regulations provide that a "proposal" exists "at that stage in the development of an action when an agency subject to the Act has a goal and is actively preparing to make a decision on one or more alternative means of accomplishing that goal and the effects can be meaningfully evaluated." 40 C.F.R. § 1508.23. CEQ's regulations also mandate that an EIS be prepared "early enough so that it can serve practically as an important contribution to the decision making process, and will not be used to rationalize or justify decisions already made." 40 C.F.R § 1502.5.

Courts have enforced those regulatory requirements in a number of instances. However, on infrequent occasions, some courts have held that an agency's thinking about a contemplated project does not amount to a proposal for NEPA purposes. That was the situation in *Kleppe v. Sierra Club*, 437 U.S. 390 (1976), where the U.S. Department of Interior had prepared a single EIS for its nationwide coal leasing program, and had also prepared separate EISs for each individual lease. The Court rejected the contention that the Department was further required to prepare a regional EIS regarding coal leasing, stating that even if the Department had "contemplated" a regional-scale coal leasing program, "the contemplation of a project and the accompanying study thereof do not necessarily result in a proposal for major federal action." *Id.*

B. What Is a Major Federal Action?

In its NEPA regulations, CEQ defined "major federal action" to include "actions with effects that may be major and which are potentially subject to federal control and responsibility." Such actions include "the circumstance where responsible officials fail to act and that failure to act is reviewable by courts or administrative tribunals under the Administrative Procedure Act or other applicable law as agency action." 40 C.F.R. § 1508.18.

CEQ's regulations provide additional clarification as to when a proposal is a major federal action. They note that federal actions tend to fall within one of four categories: (i) adoption of official policies, (ii) adoption of formal plans, (iii) adoption of programs (such as a group of actions to implement a specific policy or plan, or allocating resources to implement a statute or executive directive), and (iv) approval of specific projects. 40 C.F.R § 1508.18(b). They state that "actions" include "new and continuing activities, including projects entirely or partially financed, assisted, conducted, regulated or approved by government agencies; new or revised agency rules, regulations, plans, policies, or procedures; and legislative proposals." On the other hand, actions that do not constitute actions for NEPA purposes include funding assistance solely in the form of general revenue sharing funds and the initiation of federal enforcement actions. 40 C.F.R § 1508.18(a). CEQ has also indicated that the term "major" reinforces but does not have a meaning independent of "significantly." 40 C.F.R § 1508.27.

In many cases, an action is obviously "federal." Some examples would include a federal agency building a dam, channelizing a stream, building public housing, or designing the routes commercial airliners must take. The courts have also regularly applied the EIS requirement to projects that would be undertaken by private parties, or local or state governments, where the approval of a federal agency is essential to the project.

In other circumstances, however, the "federalness" of a project may be more difficult to determine. This question has arisen, for instance, where a highway project is fully funded by a state government but there is nonetheless involvement in the project by federal agencies. These were alleged to be the circumstances in *Southwest Williamson County Community Association, Inc. v. Slater*, 243 F.3d 270 (6th Cir. 2001), in which several federal agencies had discretion to take actions that had the potential to influence the outcome of a state-funded highway project. The U.S. Court of Appeals for the Sixth Circuit took note of a CEQ regulation that declared that a non-federally funded project may become a major federal action by virtue of the aggregate of federal involvement from numerous federal agencies, even if one agency's role in the project may not be sufficient in and of itself to create a major federal action. 40 C.F.R §§ 1508.25 and 1508.27(b). The court then concluded that "there are two alternative bases for finding that a non-federal project constitutes a 'major federal action . . . : 1) when the non-federal project restricts or limits the statutorily prescribed federal decision-makers' choice of reasonable alternatives; or 2) when the federal decision-makers have authority to exercise sufficient control or responsibility over the non-federal project so as to influence the outcome of the project.'" *Id.* Applying those tests to the specific facts in *Slater*, however, the Sixth Circuit found that neither test was satisfied, and the highway project in issue was thus not a major federal action.

Disputes sometimes also arise over whether a major federal action has been taken where an agency decides *not* to do something that it has the legal authority to do. The federal courts have taken differing approaches to resolve this issue. For example, in *Ramsey v. Kantor*, 96 F.3d 434 (9th Cir. 1996), the Ninth Circuit held that the failure of the U.S. Department of Commerce to disapprove a fishery management plan for the North Pacific Salmon was a major federal action for purposes of NEPA. In contrast, the U.S. Circuit Court of Appeals for the First Circuit opined that a failure of the U.S. Coast Guard to take any action with regard to a shipment of high-level nuclear waste from France to Japan that passed through the United States' Exclusive Economic Zone off the coast of Puerto Rico was not a major federal action requiring the preparation of an EIS. *See Mayaguezanos por la Salud y el Ambiente v. United States*, 198 F.3d 297 (1st Cir. 1999).

C. When Does a Major Federal Action Significantly Affect the Quality of the Human Environment?

CEQ's NEPA regulations divide proposals for major federal actions into three categories: (i) actions that normally require an EIS, (ii) actions that normally do not require an EIS, and (iii) actions that may or may not require an EIS. Each agency must prepare its own agency-specific regulations that define each of those categories with respect to the agency's activities. 40 C.F.R. § 1501.4.

Agency actions that normally do not require the preparation of an EIS are classified as "categorical exclusions," i.e., "a category of actions which do not individually or cumulatively have a significant effect on the human environment." 40 C.F.R. § 1508.4. The purpose of these exclusions is to help agencies reduce paperwork and avoid spending resources on unnecessary environmental assessment of agency actions that will predictably have no significant environmental impact. *See* 40 C.F.R. §§ 1500.4 and 1500.5. However, agencies that adopt categorical exclusions must provide for "extraordinary circumstances" in which a normally excluded action may have a significant environmental effect. 40 C.F.R. § 1508.4. Where such circumstances arise, an agency must prepare an EIS or an environmental assessment, and the U.S. Court of Appeals for the Ninth Circuit has held that "where there is substantial evidence in the record that exceptions to the categorical exclusion may apply, the agency must at the very least explain why the action does not fall within one of the exceptions." *California v. Norton*, 311 F.3d 1162 (9th Cir. 2002).

In addition to categorical exclusions, Congress and the federal courts have created other, specific exceptions to the EIS requirement. Thus, for example, in the Energy Supply and Coordination Act of 1974 ("ESECA"), the Federal Energy Administration was permitted to issue orders temporarily requiring the burning of coal, rather than oil or natural gas, without preparing an EIS, P.L. 93-319 § 2. More broadly, ESECA provided that "no action taken under the Clean Air Act ... shall be deemed a major federal action significantly affecting the quality of the human environment." *Id.* at § 6(b). And all actions taken by EPA under the Clean Water Act—other than providing grants or loans for the construction of sewage treatment plants and issuing discharge permits for new sources of water pollution—are expressly exempted from the EIS requirement of NEPA. 33 U.S.C. § 1371(c)(1).

Similarly, courts have concluded that certain regulatory actions required of EPA are the "functional equivalent" of an EIS, and therefore do not require the preparation of a formal statement. Thus, for example, it has been held that EPA is exempt from the duty to prepare an EIS when it promulgates Clean Air Act New Source Performance Standards, grants a permit to a TSDF under RCRA, approves or cancels the registration of a pesticide under FIFRA, and designates the critical habitat of an endangered species under the Endangered Species Act. See *Portland Cement Association v. Ruckelshaus*, 486 F.2d 375 (D.C. Cir. 1973); *Alabama ex. rel. Siegelman v. Environmental Protection Agency*, 911 F.2d 499 (11th Cir. 1990); *Merrell v. Thomas*, 807 F.2d 776 (9th Cir. 1986); and *Douglas County v. Babbitt*, 48 F.3d 1495 (9th Cir. 1995).

Where an agency action may or may not require the preparation of an EIS, the CEQ regulations require that it prepare an "Environmental Assessment," i.e., a "concise public statement" that "briefly provides sufficient evidence for determining whether or not to prepare an EIS ..." 40 C.F.R. § 1508.9(a). This document must include brief discussions of the need for the proposal, the environmental impacts of the proposed action and alternatives to it, and a listing of the agencies and persons consulted in its preparation. 40 C.F.R. § 1508.9(b).

Where an Environmental Assessment concludes that an agency proposal will have a significant effect on the human environment, a full EIS must be prepared with respect to it. On the other hand, where the Assessment determines that no significant effect on the human environment is to be expected from the agency action contemplated, the agency is required to prepare and publish a Finding of No Significant Impact ("FONSI") that briefly presents its reasons for concluding that its action will not have a significant effect on the human environment, and for which no EIS will be prepared. 40 C.F.R. § 1508.13.

CEQ's regulations define the statutory term "significantly" in terms of both the "context" and the "intensity" of a proposed agency action. "Context" means that "the significance of an action must be analyzed in several contexts, such as society as a whole (human, national), the affected region, the affected interest, and the locality." 40 C.F.R. § 1508.27(a).

Intensity refers to the severity of the impact. 40 C.F.R. § 1508.27(b). The regulations mandate that agencies take 10 factors into account in evaluating the intensity of a proposed action: (i) impacts that may be both beneficial and adverse, (ii) the degree to which the proposed action affects public health or safety, (iii) unique characteristics of the geographic area, (iv) the degree to which the effects on the quality of the human environment are likely to be controversial, (v) the degree to which the possible effects on the human environment are uncertain, (vi) whether the action is related to other actions with individually insignificant but cumulatively significant impact, (vii) the degree to which the action may adversely affect historical, scientific or cultural resources, (viii) the degree to which the action may establish a precedent for future actions with significant effects, (ix) the degree to which the action may adversely affect an endangered or threatened species or its critical habitat, and (x) whether the action threatens a violation of federal, state, or local environmental law. *Id.*

However, the U.S. Supreme Court has held that psychological damage from the mere risk of a future environmental harm is not an "environmental effect" or an "environmental impact" as to which an EIS must be prepared. *See Metropolitan Edison Co. v. People Against Nuclear Energy*, 460 U.S. 766 (1983).

Where an EIS must be prepared, the CEQ's regulations require that "connected actions" be considered together in a single EIS. These are defined as actions that "automatically trigger other actions which may require environmental impact statements, cannot or will not proceed unless other actions are taken previously or simultaneously, [or] are independent parts of a larger action and depend on the larger action for their justification." 40 C.F.R. § 1508.21(a)(1). They also direct that "cumulative actions," meaning "actions which when viewed with other proposed actions have cumulative significant impacts," must be considered together in a single EIS. 40 C.F.R. § 1508.25(a)(2).

IV. Adequacy of the Environmental Impact Statement

CEQ's NEPA regulations prescribe procedural steps that agencies must take to complete an EIS, as well as some minimal substantive criteria that an

EIS must meet. Agencies are required to begin preparing an EIS "early enough so that it can serve practically as an important contribution to the decision-making process." 40 C.F.R. § 1502.5. Once it has been determined that an EIS must be written, an agency must first decide on the range of actions, alternatives, and impacts that the EIS will consider, in a process known as "scoping." 40 C.F.R. §§ 1502.5, 1501.7, and 1508.25. As a component of scoping, the agency must solicit the participation of others, including affected state, local, and tribal governments, the proponent of the proposed action in question (if any), interested persons who might object to the action on environmental grounds (if any), and the general public. 40 C.F.R. §§ 1501.7(a)(1) and 1506.6.

After scoping is complete, the agency—often with assistance from a contractor or permit applicant—must produce a draft environmental impact statement ("DEIS"). This document must be made available to, and request comments from, the public, the project application (if any), other interested persons, other federal agencies with expertise regarding or jurisdiction over any relevant environmental impact, and appropriate environmental agencies at every level of government. *See* 40 C.F.R. §§ 1502.9, 1502.19, 1503.1, 40 C.F.R. 1503.2, and NEPA § 102(2)(C), 42 U.S.C. § 4332(2)(C). A provision of the Clean Air Act requires EPA to comment on every EIS and to evaluate the environmental effects of each action studied in an EIS. Clean Air Act § 309, 42 U.S.C. § 7609.

After receiving and considering comments on its DEIS, an agency must prepare, circulate, and file with EPA a final EIS ("FEIS"), which must include the agency's responses to the comments it received. 40 C.F.R. §§ 1502.19, 1502.9(b), and 1503.4. The agency may not take any action on the proposal that is the subject of the FEIS that would limit its choice of alternatives, or have an adverse environmental effect, until 30 days after it has published notice of the complete FEIS. At that point, however, the agency is free to make a final decision respecting its proposal for a major federal action. It must inform the public of that decision in a publicly available "record of decision," following which it may proceed to implement the action it has chosen to pursue. 40 U.S.C. §§ 1506.1, 1506.10(b)(2), and 1505.2.

Courts have long accepted the notion that plaintiffs with standing to sue may seek judicial review of the adequacy of a final environmental impact statement. Plaintiffs may base their challenges on procedural or substantive grounds, or both. In the context of such challenges, reviewing courts generally apply a "rule of reason" standard, focusing on whether the FEIS in question reflects an abuse of agency discretion. *See, e.g., Utahns for Better Transportation v. U.S. Department of Transportation*, 305 F.3d 1152 (10th Cir. 2002); and *Marsh v. Oregon Natural Resources Council*, 440 U.S. 360 (1989) (in which the U.S. Supreme Court ruled that a decision by the U.S. Army Corps of Engineers not to supplement its FEIS based on new information was not arbitrary or capricious).

V. The Interpretation Mandate of § 102(1): NEPA's Sleeping Giant

As noted above, NEPA § 102(1) provides that Congress "authorizes and directs that, to the fullest extent possible, the policies, regulations and public laws of the United States shall be interpreted and administered in accordance with the policies set forth in this [Act]." This "interpretation mandate" has received very limited application in NEPA litigation. Nonetheless, given its directive language and potentially broad reach, this provision has the potential to significantly influence federal law and policy.

One legal scholar has argued that the interpretation mandate extends to federal judges as well as Executive Branch officials. *See* Joel A. Mintz, *Taking Congress's Words Seriously: Towards a Sound Construction of NEPA's Long Overlooked Interpretation Mandate*, 38 Envt'l. L. 103 (2008). To the extent that is true, federal courts are compelled by statutory directive to interpret federal statutes and agency policies and regulations consistent with NEPA's policy of encouraging "productive and enjoyable harmony between man and his environment" and of promoting "efforts which will prevent or eliminate danger to the environment and biosphere" and stimulating "the health and welfare of man."

Even if that expansive reading of § 102(1) is not accepted by courts, however, NEPA's interpretation mandate may nonetheless be held to apply to the president and federal Executive Branch agencies and departments. Those federal institutions obviously include (but are not limited to) EPA, the Department of Interior, and other federal entities responsible for regulating environmental pollution or managing federally owned resources. If that is the case, the interpretation mandate's ultimate impact may be vast. Whether that will occur remains to be seen. Until then, NEPA § 102(1) remains a sleeping giant of federal law.

VI. Remedies for NEPA Violations

As we have seen, the U.S. Supreme Court has interpreted NEPA's primary action-forcing provision, the EIS requirement, as purely procedural. As a result of this authoritative interpretation, typical judicial remedies for procedural violations of NEPA tend to require additional procedural measures. Courts, for example, may order agencies to prepare Environmental Assessments where a categorical exclusion has been improperly used. They may direct an agency to prepare a new Environmental Assessment, or draft an EIS where a first environmental assessment is deemed inadequate; or they may require preparation of a new EIS, or a supplementary EIS, where a first EIS was procedurally flawed or incomplete.

NEPA litigation is often initiated to stop, or at least delay, a federal project that the plaintiffs believe will harm the environment. To keep such a project from becoming a *fait accompli* while their NEPA lawsuit is still pending, such plaintiffs often move for a preliminary injunction to temporarily halt the project until the legal issues before the court have been resolved. Plaintiffs who seek preliminary injunctive relief must satisfy a four-factor test. They must demonstrate that: (i) they will have an adequate remedy at law or will be irreparably injured if an injunction is not granted, (ii) the threatened injury to the plaintiff outweighs the harm the injunction may inflict on the defendant, (iii) plaintiff has at least a reasonable likelihood of success on the merits, and (iv) granting an injunction will serve the public interest. Federal Rule of Civil Procedure Rule 65. Preliminary injunctions are not granted lightly. Moreover, because of the requirement that the plaintiff prove a reasonable likelihood of success on the merits, motions for preliminary injunctions in NEPA cases often lead to a sort of "mini-trial-on-the-merits," with both plaintiffs and defendants introducing much of the evidence that would normally be offered in a plenary trial.

Checkpoints

- NEPA contains broad, strongly pro-environmental statements of purposes and policies.
- NEPA includes an "interpretation mandate" that directs that "policies, regulations and public laws of the United States" be interpreted in accordance with the Act's broad policies. This sub-section has vast potential as a mechanism for eliciting environmentally sensitive interpretations of a range of federal laws.
- The statute has several "action-forcing" provisions, the most significant of which is its requirement that federal agencies and departments prepare a detailed environmental impact statement ("EIS") for every proposal for a "major federal action" significantly affecting the quality of the human environment.
- Courts have generally held that the procedural provisions of NEPA established a "strict standard of compliance" for federal agencies. This judicial rule is intended to compel agencies to advise and inform other interested agencies, and the public, of the environmental consequences of planned federal actions, and also to aid the agency's own decisionmaking.
- EISs must be considered at every important stage of an agency's decisionmaking process.
- Citizen plaintiffs may bring suit through the Administrative Procedure Act to challenge an agency's failure to follow NEPA's procedural mandates and/or the adequacy of a final EIS.
- The U.S. Supreme Court has ruled that while reviewing courts may review agencies' compliance with EIS procedures, the substantive decisions reached by agencies following procedurally appropriate preparation of EISs—including decisions regarding possible mitigation measures—are not subject to judicial review under NEPA.
- NEPA created a Council on Environmental Quality ("CEQ") in the Executive Branch that has published regulations that guide federal agencies in the implementation of the Act.
- CEQ's regulations, and judicial interpretations, have fleshed out the meaning of the statutory phrases "major federal action" and "significantly affecting the quality of the human environment."
- "Major federal actions" generally involve federal actions that deal with the adoption of official policies, form a plan or program, or approve specific public or private projects.
- CEQ's regulations require agencies to divide their proposals for major federal actions into those that normally require an EIS, those that normally do not require an EIS, and those that may or may not require an EIS.
- Agency actions that normally do not require preparation of an EIS because they will predictably have no significant environmental impact are classified as "categorical exclusions."

- In circumstances where an agency action may or may not require preparation of an EIS, the agency must prepare a brief "Environmental Assessment" to determine whether or not to prepare an EIS.
- Environmental Assessments must lead to either the preparation of a full EIS or a "Finding of No Significant Impact."
- CEQ's regulations define the statutory term "significantly" in terms of both the context and intensity (i.e., severity of impact) of a proposed action.
- In preparing EISs, agencies must follow procedures set forth in detail in CEQ's regulations, which include "scoping" what the EIS will contain, circulating a draft EIS for comments from stakeholders, and preparing, circulating, and filing a final EIS.
- Typical judicial remedies for procedural violations of an EIS tend to require agencies to take additional procedural measures.
- NEPA litigation frequently involves motions for preliminary injunctions under Federal Rule of Civil Procedure 65. The proponents of those motions must satisfy four conditions to succeed in persuading courts to issue preliminary injunctions, including a showing that they are likely to succeed on the merits of the case. Such injunctions are not granted lightly.

Chapter 9

Endangered and Protected Species

Roadmap

- Understand how the federal government decides whether a species is threatened or endangered.
- Learn how federal agencies must investigate whether their actions might harm a protected species, and what approvals or permits the agency must obtain before it can proceed.
- Grasp how the Endangered Species Act forbids the harassment or injury of a protected species without a permit or authorization from the federal government.
- Understand the full scope of potential civil and criminal liability that may arise from violations of the Endangered Species Act, even if unintentional.
- Navigate the different tools and requirements for enforcement of the Endangered Species Act, including citizen suits and standing requirements.
- Know the basics of the Marine Mammal Protection Act, which provides important additional legal protection to certain marine cetaceans and coastal species such as seals, walruses, and polar bears.
- Learn key aspects of the Migratory Bird Treaty Act, which extends critical legal protections to migratory birds that can trigger criminal liability for actions that (even unintentionally) result in the death of protected birds.

I. Introduction

The Endangered Species Act (ESA) has a well-deserved reputation as the bulldog of environmental law. In essence, the ESA implements Congress' broad direction to protect imperiled species (both animals and plants) without regard for the economic value of the protected species. Given the increasing pace of extinction of imperiled species and the growing encroachment of human development into habitat needed by vulnerable species, the ESA will likely continue to grow in importance as a keystone federal environmental program.

This chapter provides an overview of key aspects of the federal Endangered Species Act and how its protections for certain species create legal obligations and liabilities for private parties and federal agencies. In particular, it focuses on the two basic strategies used by the ESA. The first strategy requires federal agencies to investigate how their actions might affect a protected species and, if necessary, take steps to mitigate any unavoidable harm to those species incidentally caused by the agency. Second, as the chapter explains, the ESA flatly prohibits harassing, injuring, or killing a protected species without authorization. The chapter concludes with a brief overview of two other important statutes that protect imperiled species: the Marine Mammal Protection Act and the Migratory Bird Treaty Act.

II. The Endangered Species Act

The ESA is the only comprehensive federal statute dedicated to the protection and preservation of endangered species. It sets out the sweeping goal of preserving all species, without regard to their economic value, value to the ecosystem, charismatic importance to humans, or any other characteristic or factor. All species, no matter how humble, may qualify for the ESA's protection if that species is endangered or threatened. As a result, the statute does not provide any overt framework or guidance on ranking species for protection or for choosing a particular species for triage. This approach, while laudable for promoting the broadest possible protection for imperiled species, has triggered controversy when it imposes unexpectedly large costs or substantially restricts the use of public or private property.

A. Section 4: Listing a Protected Species and Candidate Conservation Agreements

As a threshold step, before species receive protection under the ESA, the federal government must identify and list those species as threatened or endangered. The Act charges the Secretaries of Interior and Commerce with responsibility for listing species, and they in turn have delegated that duty to the U.S. Fish & Wildlife Service (F&WS) for terrestrial species and the National Marine & Fisheries Service (NMFS) for marine species and anadromous fish. These agencies must list a species as endangered if it faces "danger of extinction throughout all or a significant portion of its range."

Similarly, a species qualifies as threatened if it is "likely to become an endangered species" throughout all or a significant portion of its range. 16 U.S.C. § 1532(6), (20). To make this determination, the agencies must consider five factors: present or threatened destruction of habitat; overuse of the species for commercial, recreational, scientific, or educational purposes; disease or predation; inadequate regulations; and other natural or man-made factors that may affect the species' continued existence. 16 U.S.C. § 1533(a)(1)(A)–(E).

To designate a species as threatened or endangered, these agencies must rely solely on the "best available scientific and commercial data available." 16 U.S.C. § 1533(b)(1)(A). This language, added to the statute in 1982, creates a mandate that the federal government must rely solely on the scientific data relevant to a decision to list a species and not on any economic or policy assessment of the listing's impact.

The listing process does not rest solely within the discretion of the F&WS or NMFS. The ESA specifically authorizes citizens to petition the Secretary of Interior or of Commerce (in effect, the F&WS or NMFS) to list (or delist) a species that merits protection as endangered or threatened. 16 U.S.C. § 1533(b)(3)(A). The statute requires the Secretary to decide within 90 days whether that petition provides "substantial scientific or commercial information" to support the listing, and then find within 12 months after receiving the petition whether the action is warranted, not warranted, or warranted but precluded by other pending proposals to protect the species. 16 U.S.C. § 1533(b)(3)(A)–(B).

To create flexibility in the ESA's rather prescriptive listing process, agencies and stakeholders have begun to create an "off-ramp" through voluntarily agreeing to take steps to protect a species before it is listed as endangered or threatened. This proactive strategy allows parties to adopt a conservation plan to allow more flexibility in protecting habitats and species while allowing parallel commercial activity or personal uses of some habitat. The stakeholders and agencies will typically package their agreement into a Candidate Conservation Agreement with Assurances that sets out binding obligations on the parties to protect the species, and the F&WS or NMFS can then rely on that enforceable agreement as a basis to postpone or decline listing a particular species. U.S. Departments of Interior and Commerce, *Final Candidate Conservation Agreements with Assurances Policy*, 64 Fed. Reg. 32726–32736 (June 17, 1999); *Candidate Conservation Agreements with Assurances Policy*, 81 Fed. Reg. 95164 (Dec. 27, 2016). This policy, however, has proven controversial because some agreements have allegedly failed to provide the protections promised to their imperiled species.

In addition to identifying and listing threatened or endangered species, the agencies must also designate the habitat that those species need to survive. To be considered "critical habitat," an area must have physical or biological features that are essential to the conservation of the species, and that may require special management considerations or protections. 16 U.S.C. § 1532(5)(A)(i). The ESA directs the federal government to designate critical habitats "on the basis of the best scientific data available and taking into consideration the economic impact." 16 U.S.C. § 1533(b)(2).

Setting the boundaries of a critical habitat is one of the most important steps of the listing process because the ESA also prohibits actions that harm a protected species by destroying habitat critical to its survival. It is important to note that the Act's definition of "critical habitat" is limited to areas inhabited by the species at the time of its listing (although the F&WS or NMFS may expand that critical habitat to include unoccupied areas "essential for conservation of the species"). 16 U.S.C. § 1532(5)(a). Thus, the Act will not permit expansion of the current critical habitat used by a protected species even if it historically inhabited wide swaths of territory.

B. Section 7: Consultation and Incidental Take Permits

Once a species is formally listed as endangered or threatened, the ESA requires each federal agency to evaluate whether its actions could potentially harm that species. In particular, Section 7 of the ESA requires all federal agencies to consult with the F&WS or the NMFS to ensure that their actions will neither jeopardize the continued existence of a protected species nor result in the destruction or adverse modification of habitat critical to the species' survival. 16 U.S.C. § 1536(a)(2). This consultation process has real bite: if the agency finds that its action would jeopardize the species or its habitat, the ESA flatly prohibits the agency from undertaking the action. This requirement applies to any action by the agency, including actions "authorized, funded, or carried out" by the agency. Section 7 also requires the agency to use "the best scientific and commercial data" when it makes its jeopardy assessment.

The consultation process goes through several discrete steps. The agency that wants to act must first conduct an informal biological assessment to determine whether its action will potentially affect a protected species. If so, the agency must then consult with F&WS or NMFS to weigh the scale of that impact and identify any potential steps it can take to mitigate the risk to the species. This review, which may require the preparation of an extensive biological opinion, can take a considerable amount of time, require the collection and review of voluminous data, and result in the imposition of conditions or restrictions on the agency's project as needed to assure the species' protection.

In particular, the F&WS or NMFS may require the acting agency to adopt mitigation measures necessary to keep the proposed action from jeopardizing the species. These mitigation measures may include an Incidental Take Statement (ITS) that allows the agency to undertake its action by confirming it will not jeopardize the species overall and may potentially result in a take of some members of the species. That taking will be limited by the terms of the ITS within the biological opinion. If the biological opinion cannot identify sufficient mitigation measures to protect the species from jeopardy, however, the proposed action cannot proceed regardless of its cost or value (absent a rarely granted special waiver from the high-level interagency Endangered Species Act Committee, affectionately known as the "God Squad").

The ESA famously bars any actions that jeopardize a protected species without regard to cost or difficulty. In *Tennessee Valley Authority v. Hill*, 437 U.S. 153 (1978), the U.S. Supreme Court found that the Act barred the last steps needed to finish construction of a dam because it would flood the running stream habitat needed by the snail darter as critical habitat. Even though this outcome barred TVA from using a dam that it had largely completed at the cost of millions of dollars to benefit a species with virtually no economic value, the Court ruled that the ESA's plain language left no ambiguity in its absolute prohibition on federal agency actions that jeopardized an endangered species.

C. Section 9: Prohibition on Taking Protected Species and Habitat Conservation Plans

In addition to Section 7's consultation requirement, the ESA bars any actions that result in the "taking" of a protected species. While the ESA's consultation requirement applies solely to federal agency actions, the no-take prohibition of Section 9 casts a far broader net. It defines "take" expansively to include any action that could "harass, harm, pursue, hunt, shoot, wound, kill, trap, capture, or collect" a member of a protected species. 16 U.S.C. § 1532(19).

The breadth of Section 9's coverage, however, differs from Section 7's consultation requirement in several important ways. First, it only applies to takings of species, while Section 7 requires consultation for any action that jeopardizes a species or its critical habitat. 16 U.S.C. § 1538(a)(1)(B). Second, Section 9's prohibition on taking of protected species applies to everyone (including private citizens). In contrast, as noted above, Second 7 imposes its consultation requirement only on federal agencies. Third, Section 9 only protects *endangered* species from a "taking." Both F&WS and NMFS, however, routinely extend Section 9's protections to almost all *threatened* species as well through separate rulemakings authorized by the ESA. 16 U.S.C. § 1533(d). And last, Section 9 offers only limited protection to listed plant species. While fish and animals receive automatic coverage, plant species fall under Section 9's protective ambit only if they were removed or damaged in knowing violation of a state's laws, taken from federal land, or transported in interstate or international commerce. 16 U.S.C. § 1538(a)(2)(B), (C).

Violating Section 9 carries serious consequences. In addition to civil fines, the ESA imposes criminal liability for knowing violations of Section 9's statutory provisions as well as any regulations or permits issued under them. 16 U.S.C. § 1540(b)(1). Liability can reach up to $50,000 per violation and up to one year in prison.

It is important to note that a person can knowingly violate Section 9 without realizing that the animal taken was endangered or threatened (e.g., a hunter who knowingly shoots a crane without realizing it was protected under the ESA). Moreover, given the ESA's broad definition of "take," a person can face criminal liability for knowingly destroying or damaging critical habitat in a way that takes a protected species.

Beyond these financial penalties and potential prison terms, the ESA also empowers the government to seek forfeiture for any tools, traps, vessels, or other equipment used to violate Section 9 (a financial impact that can far exceed the daily penalties themselves). 16 U.S.C. § 1540(e)(4). Moreover, a violator can risk losing its lease, license, permits, or other agreements involved in the violation (for example, grazing rights on federal lands). 16 U.S.C. § 1540(b)(2). However, the Act does offer some enforcement relief by excluding from criminal and civil liability any offenses committed by a person acting on the good faith belief that an endangered or threatened species member threatened bodily harm to himself, a family member, "or any other individual." 16 U.S.C. § 1540(a)(3), (b)(3).

If an otherwise legal action might incidentally take a protected species, the ESA allows private parties to seek an incidental take permit (ITP) under Section 10. 16 U.S.C. § 1539(a). Obtaining an ITP can be challenging. For example, Section 10(a)(2)(A) requires an applicant for an ITP to submit a Habitat Conservation Plan (HCP) that spells out the likely size of the taking, how the applicant will seek to minimize and mitigate those impacts, what alternative steps the applicant considered but chose not to use, and any other measure that F&WS or NMFS required as "necessary and appropriate." 16 U.S.C. § 1539(2)(A)(i)–(iv). Before granting the ITP, F&WS or NMFS must find that the taking in question is incidental, that the HCP will minimize and mitigate its impacts, that the taking "will not appreciably reduce the likelihood of the survival and recovery of the species in the wild," and that the HCP will provide adequate funding for the plan. 16 U.S.C. § 1539(2)(B)(i)–(v). While developers have traditionally sought ITPs for individual development projects, some of them have recently begun to consolidate their HCPs into broad regional plans to facilitate coordinated and expedited approvals.

D. Citizen Suits and Petitions

As noted above, the ESA allows citizens to petition the F&WS and the NMFS to list species that deserve protection as either endangered or threatened. The Act, however, goes much further in empowering citizen enforcement. Like several other federal environmental statutes, the ESA authorizes any person to bring a citizen civil suit to enjoin any other person (including the United States) from violating any provision of the ESA or its implementing regulations. This authority expressly includes lawsuits to force the F&WS or NMFS to halt a taking that violates Section 9 and to compel the agencies to perform a non-discretionary duty under the ESA. 16 U.S.C. § 1540(g)(1)(A)–(C). For lawsuits to enjoin a violation, the petitioner must first give the United States 60 days' notice prior to filing the action. Failure to provide this notice is a jurisdictional flaw that cannot be cured with late notice (even if no prejudice has occurred). 16 U.S.C. § 1540(g)(2).

The citizen suit provision has evolved into one of the most effective tools to enforce the ESA's requirements. The statute, however, requires that the plaintiff file the lawsuit in federal district court. 16 U.S.C. § 1540(g)(1), (3). As a result, ESA citizen suits must satisfy the constitutional standing requirements for any action brought in an Article III federal court, and the Constitution's standing to sue limitation has served as an important threshold requirement for (and barrier to) ESA citizen suits. *See, e.g., Lujan v. Defenders of Wildlife,* 504 U.S. 555 (1992); *Native Ecosystems Council v. Marten,* 883 F.3d 782 (9th Cir. 2018).

III. The Marine Mammal Protection Act

The Marine Mammal Protection Act (MMPA) protects marine mammals from attempts to "take" them without a permit. As a result, no one can harass, feed, hunt, capture, collect, or kill any marine mammal (or part of a marine mammal) without authorization or permission. The MMPA protects far more than whales and dolphins: it shields all marine mammals from human depredation, including cetaceans (whales, porpoises, and dolphins), sirenians (manatees and dugongs), pinnipeds (seals, sea lions), walruses, sea otters, and polar bears. It protects these species, however, only when they are within the waters of the United States. By focusing solely on mammals, the MMPA acts as a complement to the Magnuson-Stevens Fishery Conservation and Management Act, which protects and manages U.S. marine fisheries.

Three federal agencies jointly implement the MMPA. The National Oceanic and Atmospheric Administration (NOAA) Fisheries Service oversees protections of dolphins, porpoises, seals, sea lions, and whales. The U.S. Fish & Wildlife Service is responsible for walruses, manatees, sea otters, and polar bears; and a third agency, the U.S. Marine Mammal Commission, supplies scientific expertise and oversees federal policy regarding human impacts on marine mammals and ecosystems. Together, the three agencies focus on providing conservation strategies aimed at promoting the well-being of the ecosystem supporting marine species, rather than individual species themselves.

The Act's broad prohibition on "takes" of marine mammals does contain exceptions. Congress specifically amended the MMPA to exclude certain activities, including—most important—some "incidental takes," where legally permissible activities result in unintentional harm to marine mammals.

One example of a permitted incidental taking includes the killing or injury of marine mammals as part of commercial fishing conducted within the federal Marine Mammal Authorization Program. Other incidental takes include non-fishing activities permitted by other federal programs, such as upstream oil and gas exploration and development, renewable energy projects, construction projects, military training and preparation, and research work. Alaska natives can also take marine mammals as part of their subsistence use or to create authentic handicrafts and clothing.

IV. The Migratory Bird Treaty Act

The Migratory Bird Treaty Act (MBTA) is one of the oldest U.S. federal environmental statutes. As its name suggests, the Act implements protections provided to migratory birds by the Migratory Bird Treaty between the United States and Canada. While those nations ratified the treaty in 1916, the United States did not incorporate its requirements into federal law until passage of the MBTA in 1918. The federal law's scope has grown through the enactment of additional treaties with Russia, Japan, and Mexico that also protect migratory birds.

The MBTA sets out a simple and broad ban on any attempt to pursue, take, hunt, capture, kill, or sell protected migratory birds without permission. 16 U.S.C. § 1703. This prohibition includes both living and dead birds (as well as their body parts), and it also forbids the importation and export of protected birds. The MBTA now extends protections to more than 800 migratory bird species, and it includes both rare birds shielded under other environmental statutes (such as the ESA) as well as common and familiar birds such as crows, ravens, and songbirds. 50 C.F.R. § 10.13.

Notably, the MBTA does not define the broad term "take," and the U.S. Fish & Wildlife Service has interpreted it via regulation as "pursue, hunt, shoot, wound, kill, trap, capture or collect" any migratory bird, including that bird's body parts, nests, or eggs. The statute broadly forbids killing "by any means or in any manner," and it imposes both felony criminal liability for "knowing" violations as well as misdemeanor criminal liability for violations without proof of "knowing" conduct. 16 U.S.C. §§ 703, 707.

The federal courts have split on how broadly to interpret the term "take." Several federal courts have given it a broad reading to include any activity that has the direct effect of killing or injuring a migratory bird. *U.S. v. Apollo Energies, Inc.*, 611 F.3d 679 (10th Cir. 2010); *U.S. v. FMC Corp.*, 572 F.2d 902 (2d Cir. 1978); *U.S. v. Moon Lake Electric Ass'n.*, 45 F. Supp. 2d 1070 (D. Colo. 1999). In contrast, several other federal appellate courts have interpreted "take" and "kill" to only encompass affirmative conduct directed against wildlife. *U.S. v. CITGO Petroleum Corp.*, 801 F.3d 477 (5th Cir. 2015); *Newton County Wildlife Ass'n. v. U.S. Dept. of Agriculture*, 113 F.3d 110 (8th Cir. 1997); *Seattle Audubon Society v. Evans*, 952 F.2d 297 (9th Cir. 1991).

The scope of these terms plays an enormous role in environmental enforcement because most major spills, upsets, or releases (particularly to water) will often injure or kill migratory birds. The U.S. Supreme Court has not yet addressed the split between the circuits on the scope of "take" under the MBTA.

In the meantime, the F&WS recently changed its interpretation of the "take of birds" to exclude activities that cause the death of birds unless those activities' underling purpose was to take migratory birds, their eggs, or their nests. Principal Deputy Director, U.S. Department of Interior Fish & Wildlife Service, *Guidance on the recent M-Opinion affecting the Migratory Bird Treaty Act*, at 1, 3 (2018). This guidance has not yet received any judicial review or legal challenge.

The MBTA empowers the U.S. Fish & Wildlife Service to authorize some types of migratory bird "takes." Pursuant to this authority, the F&WS has set up four flyway councils to review data on the population of migratory birds that transit through corridors under the councils' jurisdiction. Each council for a flyway can then authorize hunting, taking, or killing of migratory birds pursuant to regulatory authorizations or hunting permits.

Each of the bilateral treaties underlying the MBTA designate species of migratory birds as "game birds" that can be legally hunted. The MBTA delegates authority to the U.S. Secretary of the Interior to establish hunting seasons for game birds, and in turn the F&WS has decided that game birds must be a species for which there is a long tradition of hunting, as well as a population that can support such hunting. As a result, even though the MBTA classifies more than 170 species as game birds, fewer than 60 species are usually hunted each year.

The MBTA occupies an unusual place in federal environmental laws because it primarily relies on Congress' power to pass legislation to implement a treaty obligation (as opposed to the Commerce Clause) under the U.S. Constitution. As a result, the U.S. Supreme Court upheld the MTBA as a valid exercise of congressional authority created by treaty commitments even if it arguably lacked authority to regulate solely intrastate conduct involving migratory birds. *Holland v. Missouri*, 252 U.S. 416 (1920). Notwithstanding this broad expansion of Congress' authority, however, the U.S. Supreme Court found that a U.S. Army Corps of Engineers' attempt to regulate solely intrastate waters because migratory birds inhabited them raised constitutional concerns about the scope of Congress' powers under the Commerce Clause. The Court accordingly interpreted the Corps' regulatory definitions to exclude such waters thereby avoiding a statutory interpretation that might violate the U.S. Constitution. *Solid Waste Agency of Northern Cook County v. U.S. Army Corps of Engineers*, 531 U.S. 159 (2001).

Given its age, the MBTA does not expressly authorize a private right of action or any citizen suits (a relatively recent legislative invention). This statutory structure is logical since the MBTA relies solely on criminal prosecution to enforce its provisions, and it lacks any civil enforcement provision. However, the federal courts have ruled that the MBTA does allow private parties to sue federal agencies under the federal Administrative Procedure Act to enforce nondiscretionary obligations imposed by the statute. *Humane Society of the U.S. v. Glickman*, 217 F.3d 882 (D.C. Cir. 2000). Plaintiffs in such actions, however, may only seek an injunction to force compliance with the MBTA. The Act does not allow for the recovery of penalties or fines.

Checkpoints

- The Endangered Species Act protects only species that the federal government has affirmatively listed as either endangered or threatened.
- The U.S. Fish & Wildlife Service (F&WS) or the National Marine Fisheries Service (NMFS) will list a species as endangered or threatened based on the best available scientific and commercial data, but they will not base the listing decision on the economic value of the species. However, they may consider economic impacts in identifying the critical habitat that the species will require to survive.
- A federal agency may not take actions that will jeopardize an endangered or threatened species. To determine if its action will jeopardize the species, a federal agency must consult with either the F&WS or NMFS. Those agencies in turn will produce a biological opinion. If the biological opinion finds that the action will jeopardize a protected species (even with mitigation or protective actions), the federal agency is not permitted to move ahead with the action.
- If the agency's action is otherwise legal, and it only causes the incidental death of some protected species members without threatening the species overall, the agency may obtain authorization for an incidental take of the species, consistent with the biological opinion.
- Any person (including private parties and federal agencies) who knowingly causes the taking of a protected land animal or fish (and, in some cases, a plant) may face civil and criminal liability under Section 9 of the Endangered Species Act. Among other things, this prohibition includes taking a species through the destruction or impairment of critical habitat needed by the species.
- If a person will only incidentally take some protected species members as part of an otherwise legal action, he or she may seek an Incidental Take Permit that would authorize the taking. Such permits require the submission of a Habitat Conservation Plan that would assure the protection of the protected species.
- The Marine Mammal Protection Act also prohibits the taking of members of marine species (including whales, dolphins, walruses, seals, sea lions, and polar bears) in marine waters under U.S. jurisdiction. Some exceptions to this prohibition allow limited incidental takes of some species, including hunts for subsistence needs by native American tribes and scientific research.
- The Migratory Bird Treaty Act protects migratory birds, including a vast array of songbirds, waterfowl, and common birds. This Act relies on criminal liability for enforcement, and its reduced requirements for misdemeanor criminal liability makes it an important environmental enforcement tool after spills or releases that injure migratory birds.

Chapter 10

Environmental Enforcement

Roadmap

- Understand the role of self-monitoring and self-reporting in environmental enforcement.
- Learn when search warrants are required when government inspections wish to enter private property.
- Distinguish among Notices of Violation, Administrative Compliance Orders, and Administrative Penalty Orders.
- Comprehend what the government must prove in an environmental civil judicial enforcement case and what affirmative defenses may be raised in that context.
- Grasp what government prosecutors must prove in environmental criminal cases and the defenses most commonly raised by defendants in those cases.
- Know the unique procedural hurdles that must be overcome by plaintiffs in citizen enforcement actions, including the pre-filing notice statutory jurisdiction requirements, claims of mootness and statutory preclusion.

I. Introduction and Overview

Enforcement is widely recognized to be a critical component of effective environmental regulation. It provides an incentive for regulated entities to comply with applicable environmental requirements, penalizes noncompliance, deters potential violations, and creates a "level playing field" on which violating parties cannot gain a competitive advantage over firms that adhere to environmental laws.

Most environmental statutes provide a variety of enforcement mechanisms to regulatory authorities. Environmental agencies compel regulated parties to provide them with information regarding their compliance status, engage in administrative enforcement, bring civil lawsuits to redress violations, or prosecute violators in instances of environmental criminal activity. Nearly all federal environmental statutes also allow private citizens to initiate civil actions directly against parties in violation of permit conditions, administrative orders, or statutory requirements.

This chapter examines the various enforcement tools available to federal and state environmental regulators and citizen plaintiff and legal issues that arise in the environmental enforcement context. After focusing on governmental authority to obtain relevant information, we will consider, in turn, administrative, civil judicial, criminal, and citizen suit enforcement.

II. Information Gathering

Self-monitoring and self-reporting by regulated pollution sources are common and important features of environmental regulation. Such sources are frequently required to sample and analyze their own effluents and discharges for the presence and concentration of pollutants, monitor groundwater quality, and/or maintain and calibrate their pollution control equipment. They must report the results of their self-monitoring to local, state, and/or federal pollution control officials.

Self-reported data may create the basis for an administrative order or a civil judicial enforcement action by government agencies or citizens. Agencies may also use source self-monitoring reports as a basis for targeting on-site inspections. However, source self-monitoring data may not be introduced as evidence in an environmental criminal prosecution due to Fifth Amendment limitations on self-incrimination.

One question that has arisen is whether a regulated party that has self-reported the violation of an environmental standard may successfully raise the defense that its self-monitoring reports were unreliable because the source's sampling and analysis were erroneous. The U.S. Circuit Court of Appeals for the Ninth Circuit resolved that question in the negative in *Sierra Club v. Union Oil Co.*, 813 F.2d 1480 (9th Cir. 1987). Reversing the U.S. District Court, the court noted that "[A]llowing permittees to excuse their reported exceedance by showing sampling error would create the perverse result of rewarding permittees for sloppy laboratory practices. Such an approach would surely undermine the efficacy of the self-monitoring program." *Id.* The court also reasoned that allowing regulated parties to impeach their own reports by showing errors would sanction "countless additional hours of litigation and create new, complicated questions of fact for district courts to resolve." *Id.*

Environmental statutes frequently authorize representatives of environmental agencies to carry out on-site inspections at privately owned or operated facilities. In the vast majority of cases, EPA and state inspectors gain access to regulated facilities with the free consent of the owner or operator. In rare instances, however, such consent is withheld.

In cases where the owner or operator objects, the U.S. Supreme Court has held that a search warrant is constitutionally required before a government inspector may enter the private property in question. *See Marshall v. Barlow's Inc.*, 436 U.S. 307 (1978). To obtain a warrant, however, a showing of "probable cause," in the criminal law sense, is not required. Instead, the government officials may obtain a search warrant by demonstrating that the business in question was chosen for inspection on the basis of "a general administrative plan for enforcement derived from neutral sources." *Id.*

Courts, however, have recognized exceptions to the general warrant requirement that allow the government to enter private property, without either consent or a warrant, under limited conditions. Thus, environmental law enforcement officers may enter private property where "exigent circumstances" exist, e.g., during an emergency response to a spill cause by a ruptured oil pipeline. Warrantless entries to properties are also permitted where the premises are part of a "pervasively regulated industry," in which the owner or operator of a plant should have an expectation that its facility will be inspected frequently at certain times. *See, e.g., New York v. Burger*, 381 U.S. 41 (1987); *U.S. v. Biswell*, 406 U.S. 311 (1973); *Donavan v. Dewey*, 452 U.S. 594 (1981); and *In re Mullins and Pritchard, Inc.*, 549 So. 2d 872 (La. Ct. App 1989).

In addition to self-reporting and on-site facility inspections, under the "open fields doctrine" environmental regulators may collect information regarding pollution levels that is readily visible to members of the public. Thus, they may gather data on a facility from observations made off-site from a public sidewalk or nearby hill, by utilizing mapping programs or Google Earth, or by taking photographs while flying over a facility in an airplane. *See Dow Chemical v. United States*, 476 U.S. 227 (1986).

III. Administrative Enforcement

Administrative enforcement represents a large proportion of the enforcement activities of many environmental agencies. It requires less expenditure of governmental resources than do civil or criminal enforcement, and it is particularly well-suited to addressing less egregious environmental violations.

A. Notices of Violation

The least punitive administrative enforcement technique is the Notice of Violation ("NOV"), which is analogous to a traffic warning issued to a speeding automobile driver by a police officer. The NOV simply brings an environmental violation to the attention of the violator and requests compliance. Its issuance sometimes results in more or less immediate compliance. The NOV may also document a violation or a history of violations in the event that further enforcement action is needed.

At the same time, however, no legal consequences flow directly from the issuance of an NOV because all of the obligations and rights of parties that receive this Notice are determined by the law itself, and not by a notification that the law is being violated. NOVs are therefore not considered "final agency action" that subjects them to judicial review. *See, e.g., Luminant Generation Co., LLC v. U.S. EPA*, 757 F.3d 439 (5th Cir. 2015).

B. Administrative Compliance Orders

Most environmental agencies are also authorized to issue an administrative compliance order ("ACO") to require compliance with environmental requirements or compel actions that the agency considers necessary to protect the environment. The mechanism allows environmental officials to require regulated entities to achieve final compliance after taking specific interim steps, consistent with a detailed, enforceable timetable.

ACOs—which are sometimes referred to as "abatement orders" or "cease and desist orders"—may be issued unilaterally or else with the consent of a regulated party following negotiations. Because noncompliance with an ACO may result in significant monetary penalties, most parties who receive them choose to comply with their terms. However, where a party refuses to do so, ACOs are not self-executing. Environmental officials must initiate a civil judicial action to enforce an ACO in those circumstances.

In addition, the U.S. Supreme Court has ruled that, at least under the Clean Water Act, administrative compliance orders are final agency actions that are subject to "pre-enforcement review." *Sackett v. Environmental Protection Agency*, 132 S. Ct. 1367 (2012). This ruling does not apply in the context of all federal environmental statutes. Thus, for instance, administrative orders issued under CERCLA are subject to a statutory ban on pre-enforcement review. CERCLA § 113(h), 42 U.S.C. § 9613(h). Moreover, EPA does not view ACOs that address oil spills under the Clean Water Act to be reviewable before they become enforceable. *See* U.S. EPA, "Language Regarding Judicial Review of Certain Administrative Enforcement Orders Following the Supreme Court Decision in *Sackett v. EPA*" (March 21, 2013).

Parties subject to ACOs sometimes attempt to use such orders as the basis for relief from the requirements of environmental permits or other otherwise applicable environmental requirements. These attempts are typically unsuccessful. Permits have been held to be the controlling legal authority in these cases. They remain in effect until revoked, modified, or reissued; and extensive regulatory procedures—as opposed to the mere issuance of an ACO—must be followed before the terms and conditions of a permit may be modified. *See United States v. Metropolitan District Commission*, 22 ERC (BNA) 1350 (D. Mass 1985).

C. Administrative Penalty Orders

In addition to ACOs, environmental agencies are sometimes authorized to issue administrative penalty orders that directly assess specific monetary penalties against environmental violators. The rights of a party receiving a penalty order vary by jurisdiction, agency, and statute. Parties that have received such orders are typically afforded an opportunity to negotiate lower penalties than those that the agency has proposed. Where those discussions are unavailing, in some jurisdictions those parties are entitled to a hearing before an administrative law judge (ALJ) or a hearing board. In other jurisdictions, the regulated party may seek immediate judicial review of the proposed penalty amount.

At EPA, entities that receive administrative penalty orders from regional enforcement personnel have the right to an adjudicatory hearing before an ALJ. These hearings are conducted under EPA's Consolidated Rules of Practice, 40 C.F.R. pt. 22. Under these procedural rules, discovery is considerably more limited than is the case under the Federal Rules of Civil Procedure. *See* 40 C.F.R. § 22.19. Adjudicatory hearings themselves are analogous to bench trials in U.S. District Courts. However, the Federal Rules of Evidence are not strictly applied in this context.

Following a hearing in an EPA regional office, the ALJ will generally issue a written decision that may be appealed to EPA's Environmental Appeals Board (EAB). This Board is a component of the Office of the Administrator of EPA. It operates as the final, national EPA decision-maker concerning administrative proceedings.

ALJs must consider all relevant penalty policies adopted by the Agency. However, ALJs are also free to deviate from those policies where they believe that doing so is appropriate. Nonetheless, both the ALJ and EAB may, and very often do, apply pertinent EPA penalty policies in matters before them. *See M.A. Bruder and Sons, Inc.*, 10 E.A.D. 599 (EAB 2002).

IV. Civil Judicial Enforcement

Civil judicial enforcement is an approach taken by some environmental agencies in cases involving recalcitrant violators or violations that result in significant environmental harm. It is also employed in cases where an agency believes that a favorable legal precedent is needed.

A. The *Prima Facie* Case

The precise elements that the government must prove in civil enforcement cases vary from statute to statute. In typical Clean Water Act cases, for example, governmental plaintiffs must prove: (i) that a "person," (ii) discharged "pollutants," (iii) from a "point source," (iv) without an NPDES permit or in violation of requirements included in an NPDES permit. The terms "person," "pollutant," and "point source" are all specifically defined in the Act. In contrast, to prove a Clean Air Act violation, the government must demonstrate that the defendant violated a requirement of its permit, an administrative order, an emission limitation imposed in a state implementation plan, or some other applicable requirement of the statute or a federal regulation.

Typically in a civil enforcement action the government has the burden of proof by a preponderance of the evidence under a strict liability regime. Fault on the defendant's part need not be demonstrated; nor does the government need to allege or prove environmental harm to obtain civil penalties or injunctive relief. In cases that involve two or more defendants, liability is often joint and several unless a defendant can demonstrate that a remedy to be awarded by the court can be logically divided between or among the defendants based upon the relative contributions of those parties to the violations in question.

B. Defenses to Liability

In a civil enforcement action, once the government has made out a *prima face* case, affirmative defenses are usually limited and difficult to establish. Although defendants have often asserted defenses based upon a variety of constitutional provisions—from the equal protection, due process, commerce, and takings clauses to the Thirteenth Amendment (banning involuntary servitude)—these defenses have nearly always been unsuccessful. The same is usually true with regard to defenses based on the receipt of incorrect information from government employees, on laches, and on the doctrine of primary jurisdiction. *See, e.g., United States v. Sharon Steel Corp.*, 30 ERC (BNA) 1778 (N.D. Ohio 1989).

One notable exception, however, is the "fair notice defense," a defense grounded in the notion that an environmental agency's regulations did not provide regulated parties with adequate advance notice of the conduct that was required of them. In cases in which this defense is asserted, courts will sometimes apply an "ascertainable certainty" standard to determine whether a regulation has provided fair notice of its meaning to the regulated community. One U.S. Circuit Court of Appeals has articulated this test by stating: "[i]f by reviewing the regulation and other public statements issued by the agency, a regulated party acting in good faith would be able to identify, with 'ascertainable certainty,' the standards with which the agency expects parties to conform, then the agency has fairly notified a petitioner of the agency's interpretation." *General Electric Co. v. Environmental Protection Agency*, 53 F.3d 1354 (D.C. Cir. 1995).

In civil environmental enforcement cases that seek judicial imposition of civil penalties for environmental violations, a five-year statute of limitations generally applies. *See* 28 U.S.C. § 2462. However, there are important exceptions.

The five-year statute of limitations does not apply to government (or citizen) requests for injunctive relief. *See U.S. v. Telluride Co.*, 146 F.3d 1241 (10th Cir. 1998). It is also not applicable in situations of "continuing violations." *See, e.g., Sierra Club v. Johnson*, 69 ERC (BNA) 1919 (N.D. Cal. 2009) and *United States v. Reaves*, 923 F. Supp. 1530 (M.D. Fla. 1996). The five-year statute of limitations does not pertain where the parties to an environmental lawsuit have entered into a "tolling agreement" that expressly extends the limitations period. In addition, in CERCLA enforcement cases involving attempts by plaintiffs to recover the cost of removing hazardous substances, the statute in question specifically provides that the cost recovery action must be initiated within three years of *completion* of the cleanup work in question. *See* CERCLA § 113(g)(2), 42 U.S.C. § 9613(g)(2).

V. Criminal Enforcement

Nearly all federal pollution control statutes contain criminal enforcement provisions. Since the 1980s, federal environmental statutes have included felony crimes that carry the potential for imprisonment for more than 12 months. For example, under the Clean Water Act, a knowing discharge of a water pollutant without a permit carries the possibility of a fine and/or up to three years in prison. Clean Water Act § 309(c), 433 U.S.C. § 1319(c). Persons convicted of knowingly violating any requirement of a Clean Air Act State

Implementation Plan or preconstruction review requirement, or an administrative order issued under the statute, may be imprisoned for as many as five years. Clean Air Act § 113(c)(1); 42 U.S.C. § 7413(c)(1). Under RCRA, persons who knowingly treat, store, or dispose of hazardous waste without a permit may be sentenced to up to two years in prison. RCRA § 3008(d)(2), 42 U.S.C. § 6928(d)(2). Failure to report a release of a hazardous substance in excess of reportable quantities similarly carries a maximum criminal penalty of up to three years in prison (or five for repeat offenses) under CERCLA § 103(b), 42 U.S.C. § 9603(b). Moreover, where the environmental crime constitutes "knowing endangerment"—a crime that involves placing another person in imminent danger of death or serious bodily injury—three pollution control statutes (the Clean Air Act, the Clean Water Act, and RCRA) all establish maximum penalties of 15 years in prison.

Federal natural resource protection statutes also authorize stringent penalties for criminal violations. Thus, for example, under the Lacey Act—which prohibits trafficking in illegally taken plants, wildlife, and fish—illegal export, import, or commercial activities may be penalized by up to five years in prison and forfeiture of vehicles, vessels, and other property, 16 U.S.C. § 3373(d). And violations of the Migratory Bird Treaty Act, which bans unlawful killing, taking, capturing, or killing of a bird, and the unlawful transportation of a bird part, may be punished by up to two years in prison where the conduct in question is done for commercial purposes, 16 U.S.C. § 703.

Some general federal crimes set out in Title 18 of the United States Code are often also charged in cases involving criminal violations of environmental requirements. Thus, for example, indictments of defendants under the criminal provisions of federal environmental laws may contain additional counts of mail fraud, wire fraud, perjury, conspiracy, obstruction of justice, the federal RICO statute, the federal aiding and abetting statute, or some other general crime. A good illustration of the application of the aiding and abetting statute to prosecute an environmental violator—using a theory of "willful blindness" with respect to a defendant who turned a blind eye to how its hazardous waste was disposed of—can be found in *United States v. Wasserson*, 418 F.3d 225 (3d Cir. 2005).

A. Standards of Proof

Though environmental laws may define a broad range of conduct as criminal, prosecutions of potential environmental criminal defendants tend to be selective. Most environmental criminal cases involve intentional wrongful conduct by individual corporate officials and/or corporate entities themselves.

Government agencies typically reserve criminal enforcement for especially egregious cases that involve culpable conduct—as demonstrated by deliberate misconduct and/or a potential defendant's history of violations—and significant harm to human health or the environment.

The Clean Water Act, RCRA, and other federal environmental statutes have been judicially determined to be "public welfare" statutes. *See, e.g.*, *United States v. Weitzenhoff*, 35 F.3d 1275 (9th Cir. 1993), and *United States v. Hoflin*, 880 F.2d 1033 (9th Cir. 1989). As a result, proof of *mens rea* is not generally required in the prosecution of the criminal sections of environmental legislation. Instead, convictions may be obtained where the government can prove, beyond a reasonable doubt, that a defendant acted with "general intent," i.e., the defendant understood the nature of his or her conduct, but not necessarily that the defendant understood that what he or she was doing was either wrongful or in violation of the law.

Environmental crimes are often drafted to require prosecutors to demonstrate that the defendant "knowingly" violated the law. In criminal cases based upon alleged violations of these kinds of provisions, as noted, courts have generally held that the word "knowingly" connotes awareness on a defendant's part that the defendant was engaged in acts that constituted the conduct proscribed by the legal requirement that forms the basis for the prosecution. The government is generally not required to prove that the defendant was aware that his or her acts violated the law. *See, e.g.*, *United States v. International Mineral and Chemicals Corp.*, 402 U.S. 558 (1971), and *United States v. Sinskey*, 119 F.3d 712 (8th Cir. 1997).

While the vast majority of environmental criminal cases are based on statutes that employ a "knowing violation" standard, the Clean Water Act contains a unique provision that makes it a crime to "negligently" violate some of the Act's mandates. *See* Clean Water Act § 309(c)(1); 33 U.S.C. § 1319(c)(1). That standard has been interpreted as imposing liability for ordinary negligence, i.e., a failure to use such care as a reasonably prudent and careful person would use under similar circumstances, as opposed to gross negligence. *United States v. Hanousek*, 176 F.3d 116 (9th Cir. 1999).

B. Defenses to Criminal Liability

Numerous affirmative defenses may be raised in environmental criminal enforcement cases. Defendants may always challenge the government's failure to allege or prove all elements of the crime(s) charged. They may also challenge the constitutionality of the statutory provision that is the basis for the prosecution and the lawfulness of the government's investigatory activities.

Beyond this, some environmental statutes, regulations, or permits provide specific affirmative defenses to charges of environmental crimes and/ or exceptions to regulatory requirements. For example, the Clean Water Act and the Clean Air Act both create a defense in a knowing endangerment prosecution where the person endangered consented to the danger and it was a foreseeable hazard of that person's occupation. *See* Clean Water Act § 309(c)(3)(b)(ii), 33 U.S.C. § 1319(c)(3)(b)(ii), and Clean Air Act § 113(c)(5)(c), 42 U.S.C. § 7413(c)(5)(c). A party charged under CERCLA with failing to provide notice of a release of a hazardous substance may defend on the ground that their release of the substance in question was a federally permitted release. CERCLA § 103(a), 42 U.S.C. § 9603(a). Violations of permits issued under the Clean Water Act may be excused if the permittee can show that a bypass of wastewater from a treatment facility was unavoidable to prevent personal injury or severe property damage, and no feasible alternatives to the bypass were available. *See United States v. City of Toledo*, 63 F. Supp. 2d 834 (N.D. Ohio 1999).

Environmental criminal defendants often file pretrial motions to suppress evidence, attempting to exclude items or communications obtained by government enforcement officials in alleged violation of the defendant's Fourth, Fifth, or Sixth Amendment rights. Irregularities in grand jury proceedings, improper joinder of defendants, or defects in criminal indictments or informations may also be challenged in pretrial motions. *See* Federal Rule of Criminal Procedure 12(b).

Double jeopardy is a defense that may be raised in an environmental criminal case. However, courts have held that the Fifth Amendment double jeopardy clause bars only additional prosecutions by the same sovereign. The double jeopardy prohibition does not apply to separate prosecutions by separate sovereigns for the same offense. *See United States v. Price*, 314 F.3d 417 (9th Cir. 2002) and *United States v. Louisville Edible Oil Products*, 926 F.2d 584 (6th Cir. 1991). The double jeopardy clause also does not shield a defendant who has been convicted of an environmental crime from subsequent civil liability. *Hudson v. United States*, 522 U.S. 93 (1997).

Defendants sometimes raise defenses based upon claims that the statutory provisions that are the basis for the environmental criminal prosecution are too vague to provide a reasonable person with an understanding of the conduct that the statute prohibits. However, courts have only rarely found environment statutes to be void for vagueness, *See, e.g., United States v. Tuerson*, 162 F.3d 1015 (9th Cir. 1998), *United States v. Cooper*, 173 F.3d 1192 (9th Cir. 1999), and *United States v. Protex Indus, Inc.*, 874 F.2d 740 (10th Cir. 1989).

Ignorance of the law—as opposed to ignorance of a material fact—cannot provide a legal basis for an affirmative defense to a charge of an environmental crime. *See United States v. Elias*, 1999 WL1204529 (D. Idaho April 20, 1999), and *United States v. Weitzenhoff*, 35 F.3d 1275 (9th Cir. 1993). While the defenses of estoppel—also known as "reliance on public authority" or "entrapment by estoppel" and entrapment are occasionally raised as defenses in environmental criminal matters, they are very rarely successful. *See, e.g., United States v. Kapp*, 2003 WL2316408 (N.D. Ill. Nov. 6, 2003), and *United States v. Engler*, 806 F.2d 425 (3d Cir. 1986).

VI. Citizen Suit Enforcement

In addition to government agency enforcement, nearly all environmental laws may be enforced by concerned citizens and organizations. In fact, with the exception of the Federal Insecticide, Fungicide and Rodenticide Act (FIFRA), every major federal pollution control and waste statute authorizes citizens to take enforcement actions against persons who violate statutory requirements, including the conditions of permits. *See, e.g.*, Clean Water Act § 505, 33 U.S.C. § 1365; Clean Air Act § 304, 42 U.S.C. § 7604; RCRA § 7002, 42 U.S.C. § 6972; Safe Drinking Water Act § 1449, 42 U.S.C. § 300j-8; Endangered Species Act § 11(g), 16 U.S.C. § 1540(g); and CERCLA § 310, 42 U.S.C. § 9659. The government is allowed to intervene as of right in any citizen suit. And citizens who have provided a notice of intent to sue have a right to intervene in any subsequent enforcement action pursued by a government agency.

Citizen suits raise many of the same legal issues that arise in government enforcement actions. However, they also pose a set of unique questions. Citizen enforcement actions must satisfy a number of procedural requirements, including pre-filing notice, statutory jurisdiction, mootness, and statutory preclusion.

A. Notice of Intent to Sue Requirements

Practically all environmental statutory citizen suit provisions require that plaintiffs provide both the alleged violator and the government with written notice of intent to sue at least 60 days prior to the filing of a suit. *See, e.g.*, Clean Water Act § 505(b)(1)(A), 33 U.S.C. § 1365(b)(1)(A). This notice requirement is meant to give government enforcers a chance to decide whether to assume the burden of pursuing the enforcement themselves and also to allow the alleged violator the opportunity to come into compliance and avoid litigation.

One question that has arisen is whether the 60-day notice provision is a mandatory precondition to suit as opposed to a less significant statutory requirement that a trial court has discretion to disregard. Addressing this issue, the U.S. Supreme Court held that the notice and 60-day delay provisions are indeed "mandatory pre-conditions precedent" to commencing a citizen suit, requirements that district courts may not disregard at their discretion. *Hallstrom v. Tillamook County*, 493 U.S. 20 (1989). The court reasoned that disregarding the plain language of citizen suit provisions ignores the possibility that a violator or agency may change its mind as the threat of a lawsuit becomes imminent. It also noted that statutory citizen suit provisions reflect a congressional intent "to strike a balance between encouraging citizen enforcement of environmental regulations and avoiding burdening the federal courts with excessive numbers of citizen suits." *Id.*

B. Citizen Suits for Wholly Past Violations

In addition to complying with notice of intent to sue requirements, citizen suit plaintiffs must establish that the court has statutory jurisdiction. Some federal environmental statutes authorize citizen suits against any party who is "alleged to be in violation" of any standard, limitation, or order. *See, e.g.*, Clean Water Act § 505(a)(1), 33 U.S.C. § 1365(a)(1), and RCRA § 7002, 42 U.S.C. § 6972. This use of the present tense by Congress raises the question of whether the "alleged to be in violation" language authorizes citizen suits for violations that are wholly in the past. The U.S. Supreme Court resolved this issue in the negative in *Gwaltney of Smithfield, Ltd. v. Chesapeake Bay Foundation, Inc.*, 484 U.S. 49(1987).

In the *Gwaltney* case, the defendant meat-packaging plant had repeatedly violated many of the effluent limitations in its permit over several years. However, the facility gradually came into full compliance with all applicable discharge requirements before the plaintiff filed its citizen suit. Reversing rulings of the U.S. District Court and the U.S. Court of Appeals for the Fourth Circuit, the U.S. Supreme Court held that the "most natural reading" of the "to be in violation" requirement that citizen plaintiffs must allege "a state of either continuous or intermittent violation—that is, a reasonable requirement that a past polluter will continue to pollute in the future." *Id.* The Court expressed concern that permitting citizen suits for wholly past violations could undermine the "supplementary role" envisioned for the citizen suit, which it indicated was intended "to supplement rather than supplant government action." *Id.* In the Court's view, doing that would also "render incomprehensible" the statute's 60-day notice requirement, which the Court stated was intended to give alleged violators the chance to bring themselves into compliance and render a citizen suit unnecessary. *Id.*

C. Mootness

Mootness is a jurisdictional issue that may be raised at any point in a judicial proceeding, either by the parties or by the court itself. Under the doctrine of mootness, a properly filed case may generally become moot if the action complained about by the plaintiff ceases, or if it is no longer possible for the court to award effective relief to the plaintiff.

At what point in a citizen suit does compliance by the defendant render that lawsuit moot? In the leading case that considered this issue, the defendant argued that the plaintiff's citizen suit claim for civil penalties was moot because it had voluntarily come into substantial compliance with its Clean Water Act discharge permit after the plaintiff's complaint had been filed and it had later permanently closed the facility at which its permit violations had occurred. The Supreme Court rejected that contention. *See Friends of the Earth, Inc. v. Laidlaw Environmental Services (TOC), Inc.*, 528 U.S. 167 (2000). The Court declared that "a defendant claiming that its voluntary compliance moots the case bears a formidable burden of showing that it is absolutely clear the allegedly wrongful behavior could not be expected to recur." *Id.* The Court noted that by the time mootness becomes an issue, the case has been brought and litigated, often for years. Thus "to abandon the case at an advanced stage may prove more wasteful than frugal." *Id.*

D. The Diligent Prosecution Bar

Nearly all environmental citizen suit provisions bar citizen enforcement where a government agency is "diligently prosecuting" a civil enforcement action. *See, e.g.*, Clean Air Act § 304(b)(1), 42 U.S.C. § 7604(b)(1). The Clean Water Act further provides that citizen suit enforcement is barred if EPA is diligently prosecuting an administrative enforcement action, or else a state agency is doing the same thing when acting under a law that is comparable to EPA's scheme for administrative enforcement. Clean Water Act § 309(g)(6), 42 U.S.C. § 1319(g)(6).

One issue that has been extensively litigated, with differing results in different courts, is what governmental enforcement activity constitutes "diligent prosecution." In general, government enforcement actions are presumed to be diligent. However, such actions are not *ipso facto* diligent; and courts have considered various factors to be indicia of diligence. These factors include: (i) whether the government sought compliance with the same standard invoked by the citizen suit, (ii) whether the government monitored the polluter's activities, or otherwise enforced the requirements at issue, (iii) whether, from the time of settlement with the polluter until commencement of the citizen suit, the penalties assessed by the government removed the polluter's economic benefits from violating the law, (iv) how the penalties obtained by the government compared with penalties imposed by the government for similar violations, and (v) the likelihood that the violations in question will continue notwithstanding the polluter's settlement with the government. *Citizens Legal Envt'l. Action Network v. Premium Std. Farms, Inc.*, 2000 WL220464 (W.D. Mo.).

Checkpoints

- Self-monitoring and self-reporting of their concentrations of effluents and discharges and related matters by regulated pollution sources are common and important features of environmental regulation.
- Regulated parties that have self-reported violations of an environmental standard may not excuse their reported noncompliance by showing sampling or laboratory errors.
- Where owners or operators of regulated sources of pollution object to the entry of a government inspector onto their facility, the government must usually obtain a search warrant. Such a warrant may be based upon a showing that the business in question was selected for inspection based upon a general administrative plan for enforcement derived from neutral sources.
- Administrative enforcement represents a large proportion of the enforcement activities of many agencies.
- Notices of Violation are warning documents that simply bring an environmental violation to the attention of the violator and request compliance.
- Administrative Compliance Orders are enforceable orders that require regulated parties to achieve compliance with environmental requirements consistent with a detailed timetable.
- Administrative Penalty Orders are used to directly assess specific monetary penalties against environmental violators. The rights of parties who receive such orders vary by jurisdiction, agency, and statute.
- The precise elements that the government must prove by a preponderance of evidence in a civil enforcement case vary from statute to statute.
- Typically, environmental statutes establish a regime of strict liability and the government need not prove environmental harm to make out a *prima facie* case.
- In civil enforcement actions, affirmative defenses are usually limited and difficult to establish.
- Where the government seeks civil penalties for environmental violations, a five-year statute of limitations generally applies, although there are some specific exceptions.
- Since the 1980s, most federal environmental statutes have included felony crimes that carry the potential for fines and imprisonment for more than 12 months.
- Prosecutors sometimes also charge general federal crimes in cases that involve alleged environmental crimes.
- Several federal environmental statutes have been deemed public welfare statutes. *Mens rea* need not be proven by government when it criminally enforces those statutes.

- Where environmental statutes require proof that a defendant "knowingly" violated the law, courts have held that the statutory term "knowingly" simply connotes awareness on a defendant's part that the defendant engaged in the prohibited acts that formed the basis for the criminal prosecution.
- Numerous affirmative defenses may be raised in environmental criminal enforcement cases, from challenges to the statute's constitutionality to entrapment, double jeopardy, statutorily created defenses, and others.
- The Fifth Amendment double jeopardy clause has been held to bar only additional prosecutions by the same sovereign. The clause does not bar separate federal and state prosecutions for the same environmental offense.
- Plaintiffs in citizen enforcement suits must satisfy a number of procedural requirements, including a demonstration of standing to sue, a pre-filing notice, statutory jurisdiction, the absence of mootness, and statutory preclusion.
- Nearly all environmental statutory citizen suit provisions require that citizen plaintiffs provide both the alleged violator and government officials with a written notice of intent to sue at least 60 days before filing suit. This notice requirement has been deemed a mandatory precondition to suit.
- Where a federal statute authorizes citizen suits against a party "alleged to be in violation" of an environmental requirement, citizen plaintiffs must allege either continuous or intermittent violations. Under those circumstances, citizen suits for wholly past violations are not permitted.
- The U.S. Supreme Court has held that defendants in environmental citizen enforcement cases raising a defense of mootness have a "formidable burden" of showing that it is "absolutely clear" that their alleged noncompliance will not recur.
- Nearly all environmental statutory citizen suit provisions bar citizen suits where the defendant can demonstrate that a government agency is "diligently prosecuting" the defendant for the same violation.

Chapter 11

Environmental Litigation and Pertinent Administrative Law

Roadmap

- Learn the standards courts use in lawsuits to block or delay environmentally damaging projects.
- Understand the concept of "hard look review" and its applicability in environmental suits.
- Comprehend "*Chevron* deference" and grasp how and when it is applied.
- Learn how federal and state courts apply the doctrine of standing to sue in environmental lawsuits by NGOs and concerned citizens, affected commercial interests, and state governments.
- Understand how the attorneys' fee provisions of environmental statutes have been interpreted.
- Comprehend the "lodestar method" used in the federal courts to determine the appropriate amount of attorneys' fees to be awarded to lawyers for prevailing parties in certain environmental litigation.
- Grasp the circumstances in which courts will and will not grant injunctive relief in environmental cases.

I. Introduction and Overview

Environmental law generates controversy. Its implementation frequently arouses strong passions among interested parties—parties that perceive (often correctly) that much is at stake in the outcomes of environmental disputes. As a result, environmental organizations and other nongovernmental organizations ("NGOs"), government agencies, private companies, trade associations, property owners, and other entities often resort to litigation in hopes of obtaining the results they desire through the courts.

Environmental lawsuits vary. They are sometimes attempts by concerned citizens to halt or modify construction projects—undertaken by government agencies or private developers—that will or may destroy the natural environment, disrupt a neighborhood, or threaten public health.

Another common type of environmental litigation is a lawsuit seeking judicial review of agency rulemaking that is seen as either too lax or too strict, or as an infringement of a person's constitutional rights. Lawsuits of this type are generally referred to as "pre-enforcement review" or "statutory review," and they are typically grounded in provisions of federal legislation that expressly permit the initiation of such suits, within a specific period, in a U.S. Circuit Court of Appeals.

Other environmental lawsuits seek judicial review of agency actions and programs under the federal Administrative Procedure Act ("APA"), usually in a U.S. District Court. This kind of judicial review, known as "non-statutory review," is most often based upon the APA's "arbitrary and capricious, or otherwise not in accordance with the law" standard. Lawsuits that challenge alleged agency failures to comply with the provisions of the National Environmental Policy Act ("NEPA")—which are discussed separately in this book's chapter on NEPA—also fall within the non-statutory review rubric. So, too, do numerous challenges to a wide variety of agency actions.

This chapter begins with a focus on environmental litigation that seeks judicial review of government agency actions. It then turns to two administrative law issues that have long had considerable practical importance in environmental lawsuits: standing to sue and the awarding of attorney's fees. Finally, we will consider the circumstances under which courts will or will not issue temporary or permanent injunctions in environmental litigation. Litigation to enforce environmental requirements is treated separately in Chapter 10 above.

II. Judicial Review of Agency Actions

A. Lawsuits to Block Controversial Projects

As mentioned above, lawsuits to block, delay, or alter planned public or privately sponsored projects that may harm the environment are an important kind of environmental litigation. The substantive basis for these suits is frequently the legislation under which an agency is proceeding. Statutory provisions that require agencies to adhere to environmentally protective procedures, or statutes under which an agency is authorized to grant a permit to a developer or manufacturer, are also often the legal foundations on which these lawsuits are constructed.

One of the earliest—and most influential—lawsuits to halt a proposed project was *Scenic Hudson Preservation Conference v. Federal Power Commission*, 354 F.2d 608 (2d Cir. 1965). That case involved a challenge by conservation organizations and several towns to a utility company's plan to build a hydroelectric pumped storage plant along a particularly scenic stretch of the Hudson River in New York State. The pumped storage plant was to be used to generate electricity during "peak load periods," when the public demand for electricity was highest. Among other things, the plaintiffs specifically sought to set aside a license to construct this facility that had been issued to the utility company by the Federal Power Commission ("FPC").

Noting that the Federal Power Act only authorized the FPC to license facilities that generate electricity where the project to be licensed is "best adapted to a comprehensive plan for improving or developing a waterway . . . for beneficial public uses, including recreation purposes," the U.S. Court of Appeals for the Second Circuit held that the FPC had failed to weigh the conservation of natural resources, the maintenance of natural beauty, and the preservation of historic sites before issuing the construction license in question. The court also found that the Commission had failed to satisfy a duty to give full consideration to alternative plans, including the use of gas turbines and interconnected power, as alternatives to the proposed pumped storage project, nor did the FPC consider the adequacy of protective devices to protect the fish resources of the Hudson River. The Second Circuit therefore set aside the utility's construction license, and remanded the matter to the FPC for further proceedings.

Another important, and paradigmatic, lawsuit to halt environmentally damaging development was *Citizens to Preserve Overton Park v. Volpe*, 401 U.S. 402 (1971). There the plaintiffs—private citizens as well as conservation associations—challenged the approval of federal funding to construct a six-lane expressway through a public park near the center of Memphis, Tennessee. The U.S. Supreme Court barred the U.S. Department of Transportation from approving and funding the highway project in question. The Court based its decision on two federal statutory provisions. Those statutory directives prohibited the Department from authorizing the use of federal funds to finance the construction of highways through public parks if a "feasible and prudent" alternative route existed and, if no such alternative existed, only if there had been "all possible planning to minimize harm" to the park. *Id.* As the Court interpreted those provisions, Congress had intended that protection of parkland was to be given "paramount importance," and the Secretary of Transportation could not lawfully approve the destruction of parkland unless he found that "alternative routes present unique problems." *Id.*

The Court applied the arbitrary and capricious test of the Administrative Procedure Act to the Secretary's actions. It held that, to approve his decisions under that test, a reviewing court would have to find that the Department's decisions had been based on "a consideration of the relevant factors" and did not reflect "a clear error of judgment." The court opined that although a reviewing court is not empowered to substitute its own judgment for that of an administrative agency, its inquiry into the facts is to be "searching and careful." Applying those criteria, the Court concluded that the administrative record in this case—a set of litigation affidavits—was simply too "bare" to allow for appropriate judicial review. It thus remanded the case to the U.S. District Court for further consideration.

The *Overton Park* case is often pointed to as an example of what has been called "hard look review." As the Court's opinion reflects, hard look review is a demanding approach. It encourages careful agency preparation of a complete record in support of whatever decision an agency reaches. It also requires that administrative agencies show that they have considered all factors that may be relevant to their determination, and that they have avoided any clear errors of judgement.

Hard look review was widely adopted by courts in their reviews of agency decision making in the 1970s. It is still employed today by courts in a number of circumstances. However, some courts take a far more deferential approach to agency determinations, accepting final agency actions in most, if not all, instances.

B. Lawsuits Challenging Promulgated Regulations

Chevron U.S.A v. Natural Resources Defense Council, 467 U.S. 839 (1984), is an oft-cited decision of the U.S. Supreme Court that reflects a far more deferential attitude toward agency decisionmaking than was the case in the *Scenic Hudson* and *Overton Park* cases. At issue in *Chevron* was an EPA Clean Air Act regulation that reflected what was known as "the bubble policy." This regulation allowed states to treat all pollution-emitting devices within the same existing industrial sources in a dirty air (nonattainment) area as though they were encased within a single bubble. Owners and operators of such plants were permitted to install or modify one piece of equipment without violating the conditions of their Clean Air Act permits, as long as the alteration would not increase the total emissions coming from the plant.

Reversing a decision of the U.S. Court of Appeals for the D.C. Circuit, the Supreme Court upheld the applicability of EPA's bubble policy to existing sources in nonattainment areas. In doing so, the Court established an influential two-step process for judicial review of an agency's construction of a statute the agency is charged with administering. In "step one" of the review process, the reviewing court must determine "whether Congress has directly spoken to the precise question at issue." If so, the court, as well the agency, must give effect to the intent of Congress.

However, if a reviewing court determines that Congress has not directly addressed the precise question at issue, the court must proceed to the second step of its review. It must inquire whether the agency's administrative interpretation of the statute is a "permissible construction." In that event, the reviewing court must defer to the agency's statutory interpretation. *Id.*

Applying what came to be known as "*Chevron* deference" to the facts, the Supreme Court concluded that Congress did not have a specific intention as to the applicability of the bubble policy. It then held that EPA's application of that policy to existing sources in dirty air regions represented "a reasonable accommodation of the manifestly competing interests" of environmental protection and reasonable economic growth, and was a "reasonable choice for the agency to make." *Id.*

The *Chevron* decision has been widely cited by lower federal courts as a basis for deferring to administrative agency decisions. Nonetheless, there is evidence that the case has frequently been ignored by the U.S. Supreme Court itself in its subsequent decisions. *See* Thomas W. Merrill, *Judicial Deference to Executive Precedent*, 101 YALE L.J. 969 (1992), and Thomas W. Merrill, *Textualism and the Future of the* Chevron *Doctrine*, 78 WASH. U.L.Q. 351 (1994).

One case in which the *Chevron* doctrine appears to have been honored more in the breach than in actuality is *Michigan v. Environmental Protection Agency*, 135 S. Ct. 2699 (2015). The *Michigan* case concerned an attempt by EPA to regulate hazardous air pollutant emissions from power plants. Toward the beginning of its regulatory development process, EPA made a finding that the regulation of hazardous pollution from power plants was "appropriate and necessary." The agency declined to take the cost of that regulation into account at that preliminary point, however, explaining instead that EPA would in the future do so when it determined specific emissions limits, and that it would explore regulatory approaches "allowing for least cost solutions."

The Supreme Court nonetheless concluded that it was "unreasonable" for EPA to have read the Clean Air Act to mean that cost was irrelevant to the Agency's initial decision to regulate power plants. Instead, in the Court's view, EPA "must consider cost—including, most importantly, cost of compliance—before deciding whether regulation is appropriate and necessary." *Id.*

III. Standing to Sue in Environmental Cases

Standing to sue ("standing") is a long-standing, and perennially important, issue in environmental litigation. The underlying purpose of the standing-to-sue doctrine is to prevent collusive lawsuits, and to ensure a truly adversarial process that will sharpen the legal arguments presented to the judiciary.

In the federal courts, the question of standing involves constitutional limitations on federal court jurisdiction that stem from the "case or controversy" requirement of Article III of the Constitution. As the courts have construed that requirement, a plaintiff must demonstrate that the plaintiff has suffered a concrete, particularized "injury in fact," that the plaintiff's injury is "fairly traceable" to the actions of the defendant, and that the plaintiff's injury will likely be redressed by a favorable decision. In addition, to be granted standing to sue in the federal courts, a plaintiff must satisfy a "prudential principle," i.e., the plaintiff's grievance must arguably fall within the "zone of interests" protected or regulated by the statutory provision or constitutional guarantee involved in the suit. *See, e.g., Bennett v. Spear,* 520 U.S. 154 (1997).

The standards pertaining to standing to sue in state court litigation vary from jurisdiction to jurisdiction. However, in many states, to obtain standing plaintiffs must at least show they have been "specially injured," i.e., harmed to a greater extent than other members of the public, and/or that the harm they suffered was economic in nature.

In environmental litigation, the issue of standing to sue has arisen in several contexts. The standing doctrine has been applied where the plaintiff is a nongovernmental organization (NGO), civic or religious organization, or concerned individual citizen. Standing to sue has also been an issue in environmental lawsuits initiated by parties with a commercial or pecuniary interest in the outcome of an environmental suit and in environmental lawsuits filed by sovereign states.

A. Standing to Sue in Lawsuits by NGOs and Citizens

The basic framework regarding the application of standing to sue in NGO-initiated environmental litigation was established by the U.S. Supreme Court in the landmark case of *Sierra Club v. Morton,* 405 U.S. 727 (1972). In that case, the plaintiff was an environmental organization that sought to enjoin the U.S. Forest Service from proceeding with a plan to turn an environmentally valuable area of great natural beauty in the Sierra Nevada Mountains into a major development complex. Addressing the issue of standing, the

Supreme Court first ruled that aesthetic and environmental well-being are "important ingredients of the quality of life in our society," and that harm to environmental interests is a "cognizable interest" that may amount to an injury in fact sufficient to lay the basis for standing. *Id.*

At the same time, however, the Court cautioned that mere organizational interest in an environmental problem, no matter how qualified a plaintiff organization may be in evaluating the problem, is not sufficient to render the organization adversely affected or aggrieved and thus eligible to bring suit. Instead, a plaintiff organization is required to show that at least some of its members make use of the natural resource that is allegedly threatened by the defendants. *Id.*

In subsequent cases, the Supreme Court placed certain additional limitations on the requirement that members of a plaintiff NGO be directly affected by alleged environmental harm. In *Lujan v. Defenders of Wildlife,* 504 U.S. 555(1992), the plaintiff filed a lawsuit challenging a regulation of the U.S. Department of Interior that provided that the Endangered Species Act—which generally requires federal agencies to ensure that their actions will not jeopardize the continued existence of any endangered or threatened species—does not apply to agency actions taken in foreign countries. In attempting to establish standing to sue, the plaintiff had submitted affidavits from two of their members averring that the affiants had traveled to two foreign countries and observed the habitats of specific species endangered by development projects that were funded by federal agencies. The affidavits indicated while that the plaintiff's members had no immediate plans to return to the countries they had visited, they would do so at unspecified future times in order to observe the same endangered species, and that the governmental actions they challenged prevented them from doing so.

The Supreme Court noted that to establish that they have suffered an injury in fact, plaintiffs must show an invasion of a legally protected interest that is "concrete and particularized," and "actual or imminent," as opposed to merely "conjectural" or "hypothetical." *Id.* Applying that principle, the Court found that the plaintiff's members' affidavits were not sufficient to demonstrate that the affiants were likely to suffer any cognizable injury-in-fact. The Court opined that "[T]he affiants' profession of an intent to return to the places they had visited before—where they will presumably, this time, be deprived of the opportunity to observe animals of the endangered species—is simply not enough. Such 'someday' intentions—without any description of *when* the someday will be—do not support a finding of the 'actual or imminent' injury that our cases require." *Id.*

The Supreme Court's attitude toward NGOs' standing to sue appears to have relaxed to an extent, however, in *Friends of the Earth v. Laidlaw Environmental Services (TOC)*, 528 U.S. 167 (2000). In *Laidlaw*, the plaintiff brought a citizen suit under the Clean Water Act to redress the defendant's discharges of mercury to a river, in violation of limitations contained in the defendant's permit. Because the defendant had achieved compliance with the mercury limits permit after the case was filed, the U.S. District Court declined to issue an injunction. However, the trial court did impose a civil penalty to sanction the defendant's previous noncompliance with its permit. The U.S. Circuit Court of Appeals for the Fourth Circuit vacated the District Court decision, ruling that since the defendant had ultimately complied with its permit the case had become moot, and, moreover, civil penalties payable to the government would not redress any injury the plaintiffs had suffered. *Id.*

The U.S. Supreme Court disagreed. Reversing the Fourth Circuit, the Court distinguished the *Lujan* case on its facts since *Laidlaw* involved no "someday" intentions to visit foreign countries. The Court held that "civil penalties may serve, as an alternative to an injunction, to deter further violations and thereby redress the injuries that prompted a citizen suitor to commence litigation." *Id.*

In *Laidlaw*, the plaintiff had filed affidavits from several of its members indicating concerns about the affiants' recreational, aesthetic, and economic interest that stemmed from the defendant's pollution. The Supreme Court found that those affidavits "adequately documented injury in fact."

The court also rejected the defendant's mootness defense, concluding that it was not absolutely clear that the defendant's permit violations were not reasonably likely to recur. *Id.*

B. The Standing to Sue of Affected Commercial Interests

The application of the standing-to-sue doctrine to parties whose commercial interests are allegedly affected by environmentally protective requirements was considered by the U.S. Supreme Court in *Bennett v. Spear*, 520 U.S. 154 (1997). The *Bennett* case involved a citizen suit challenge by two Oregon irrigation districts and two ranches to a U.S. Fish and Wildlife Service Endangered Species Act Biological Opinion. The Opinion in question would have compelled the Bureau of Reclamation to maintain certain lakes and reservoirs in a federal reclamation project at minimum water levels so as to protect the continued existence of two endangered species of fish. The plaintiffs claimed that the Service had failed to base its Biological Opinion on "the best scientific and commercial data available," as required by the statute, and that they would be harmed economically if the Opinion was not overturned.

In its analysis of the standing-to-sue issue, the Supreme Court focused primarily on whether the plaintiff's claim fell with the zone of interests protected by the Endangered Species Act. The Court answered that question in the affirmative, reasoning that the best scientific and commercial data provision of the statute was intended, at least in part, "to avoid needless economic dislocation produced by agency officials zealously but unintelligently pursuing their environmental objectives," and "to prevent uneconomic (because erroneous) jeopardy determinations." *Id.* As a result, the Court concluded, the plaintiffs' economic claims fell within the Act's protected zone of interests, and they had standing to sue. *Id.*

C. The Standing to Sue of Sovereign States

Do sovereign states have standing to challenge a federal agency's interpretation of a federal statute? This question was raised in the landmark case of *Massachusetts v. EPA*, 549 U.S. 497 (2007), a lawsuit by multiple plaintiffs, including a group of states, that sought to overturn a decision by EPA not to regulate greenhouse gas emissions from motor vehicles.

The U.S. Supreme Court noted that the Commonwealth of Massachusetts had alleged that, unless federally regulated, emitted greenhouse gases would cause climate change that would affect Massachusetts' sovereign territory. The Court opined that the Commonwealth's desire to protect its own territory was "well founded," and demonstrated that its stake in the outcome of the case was sufficiently concrete to give Massachusetts a sound basis for standing to sue. The court declared that "EPA's steadfast refusal to regulate greenhouse gas emissions presents a risk of harm to Massachusetts that is both 'actual' and 'imminent' . . . There is, moreover, a 'substantial likelihood that the judicial relief requested' will prompt EPA to take steps to reduce that risk." *Id.*

In its opinion, the Supreme Court emphasized what it termed the state's "special position and interest," stating that "[i]t is of considerable relevance that the party seeking review here is a sovereign State and not . . . a private individual." *Id.* The Court further declared that given "Massachusetts' stake in protecting its quasi-sovereign interests, the Commonwealth is entitled to special solicitude in our standing analysis." *Id.*

IV. Attorneys' Fees in Environmental Litigation

The questions of how attorneys are to be compensated for their legal work in environmental cases, and who is to bear the costs of their services, are of obvious practical significance for environmental litigants and their lawyers. Federal environmental statutes vary in their attorneys' fee provisions. Some statutes grant trial courts broad discretion to award fees to lawyers whenever the court finds that a fee award is "appropriate." Other environmental legislation, in contrast, only permits the awarding of attorneys' fees to lawyers for prevailing, or substantially prevailing parties.

In *Ruckelshaus v. Sierra Club*, 463 U.S. 680 (1983), the U.S. Supreme Court considered whether it could be deemed "appropriate," within the meaning of the Clean Air Act's attorneys' fees provision, to award attorneys' fees to a party that had achieved no success on the substantive merits of a case. The Court firmly rejected that notion. The question arose in the context of an unsuccessful challenge by two NGOs to an EPA regulation limiting sulfur dioxide emissions from coal-fired power plants. Notwithstanding the plaintiffs' lack of success on the merits, the U.S. Court of Appeals for the D.C. Circuit awarded them attorneys' fees. The Supreme Court reversed that judgment. In doing so, the Court took note of the "American Rule," under which even a prevailing litigant is not entitled to collect a reasonable attorney's fee from a losing party. It reasoned that if a *prevailing* party cannot receive attorneys' fees, it is even less appropriate for a court to award such fees to a claimant who has not succeeded in any respect in a lawsuit.

Following the *Ruckelshaus* decision, Congress adopted a "prevailing or substantially prevailing party" standard in fashioning the attorneys' fee award sections of several environmental statutes. *See, e.g.*, RCRA § 7002(e), 42 U.S.C. § 6972(e); Clean Water Act § 505(d), 33 U.S.C. § 1365(d); and CERCLA § 310(f), 42 U.S.C. § 9659(f). Under those statutes, plaintiffs must now therefore succeed in some aspect of their environmental suit to be eligible for an attorneys' fee award.

Assuming a plaintiff in an environmental lawsuit has succeeded in whole or substantial part on the merits of the case, what is the appropriate way to measure the sum of money that party is reasonably entitled to receive in an attorneys' fee award? The U.S. Supreme Court addressed this question in *City of Burlington v. Dague*, 505 U.S. 557(1992).

In *Dague*, the plaintiff had retained his attorney on a contingency fee basis to pursue a lawsuit under the Solid Waste Disposal Act. After the plaintiff had substantially prevailed in the suit, the U.S. District Court based an attorney's fee award, in part, on the fact that the plaintiff's lawyer had taken the case on a contingency fee basis. A U.S. Circuit Court of Appeals affirmed that award, but the U.S. Supreme Court reversed, ruling that the plaintiff was only entitled to an attorneys' fee based upon the lodestar method, i.e., the product of reasonable hours times a reasonable rate. Enhancement for contingency fee arrangements is not permitted. *Id.*

In its rationale, the Court stated that it had established a "strong presumption" that a lodestar-based fee represents a reasonable attorneys' fee. It reasoned that "contingency enhancement would make the setting of fees more complex and arbitrary, hence more unpredictable, and hence more litigable." *Id.* The Supreme Court also observed that "[a]n attorney operating on a contingency-fee basis pools the risks presented by his various cases: cases that turn out to be successful pay for the time he gambled on those that did not. To award a contingency enhancement under a fee-shifting statute would, in effect, pay for the attorney's time (or anticipated time) in cases where his client does not prevail." *Id.*

V. Injunctive Relief in Environmental Litigation

One question that recurs in environmental lawsuits is whether the plaintiff is entitled to injunctive relief. An injunction is an equitable remedy, the basis for which is generally an irreparable injury to the plaintiff, the absence of legal remedies, a balancing of the likely hardships to the parties from the granting of an injunction, and service or disservice to the public interest if an injunction is awarded.

In *Tennessee Valley Authority v. Hill,* 437 U.S. 153 (1978), the U.S. Supreme Court enjoined the completion of a mostly constructed federal dam project. The Court noted that an endangered species of fish, the snail darter, would be made extinct if the dam project was completed. It cited a provision of the Endangered Species Act that requires all federal agencies to insure that their actions do not jeopardize the continued existence of any endangered species; and it construed that provision as a "flat ban" on the destruction of the critical habitats of endangered species. In the Court's view, refusal to enjoin the dam would have ignored the explicit provisions of the Endangered Species Act. As the Supreme Court saw it, Congress had chosen the snail darter over the dam; and only an injunction could vindicate the clear objectives of that Act. *Id.*

The Court took a rather different approach to the awarding of injunctive relief, however, in *Weinberger v. Romero-Barceló*, 456 U.S. 305 (1982). In that lawsuit the plaintiffs had sought to enjoin the U.S. Navy from conducting weapons testing and training operations off of a small island near Puerto Rico. The Navy's activities involved the accidental and intentional bombing of water targets. The U.S. District Court found that the Navy had violated the Clean Water Act, and ordered the Navy to apply for a Clean Water Act discharge permit with regard to its operations. However, the District Court further concluded that granting an injunction against the Navy's operations while its permit application was pending would cause "grievous and perhaps irreparable harm, not only to the defendant Navy, but to the general welfare of this Nation;" and that the Navy's "technical violations" were not causing any "appreciable harm" to the environment. *Id.*

The U.S. Court of Appeals for the First Circuit, citing the *Tennessee Valley Authority v. Hill* decision of the Supreme Court, vacated the District Court's order and remanded the case with instructions that the lower court order the Navy to cease violating the Clean Water Act and discontinue its testing and training operations until a permit was issued. The Supreme Court, however, reversed that judgment and reinstated the District Court's considerably more limited injunction.

In its rationale, the Court distinguished *Tennessee Valley Authority v. Hill* on the basis that the Clean Water Act allowed the trial court a choice of remedial options that had not been available in the *Hill* case under the Endangered Species Act. In the court's opinion, the statute at issue in *Weinberger* did not anticipate that all unpermitted discharges would be immediately enjoined. Instead, the Court opined, "a federal judge sitting as chancellor is not mechanically obligated to grant an injunction for every violation of the law." Instead, in cases such as *Weinberger*, courts may (and should) exercise their discretion flexibly to do justice between the litigants. *Id.*

Checkpoints

- In lawsuits to slow or halt projects that are alleged to harm the environment, courts will sometimes apply "hard look review." This judicial approach requires agencies to justify their actions by preparing a complete administrative record that demonstrates that the agency has carefully considered all relevant factors and avoided clear errors of judgement.
- In conducting hard look review, courts may not substitute their own views for those of the defendant agency. However, reviewing courts must make a "searching and careful" review of the factual basis for the agency's decision, and they must remand the matter to the agency if they determine that it has made clear errors of judgment.
- The federal courts generally take a relatively deferential posture when they review agency interpretations of a statute that the agency is charged with administering. When Congress has spoken directly to the precise question at issue, a reviewing court (and the agency) must give effect to Congress's intent.
- Where Congress has not spoken directly to the question at issue, however, a reviewing court must defer to the statutory interpretation of the implementing agency as long as that interpretation is permissible and reasonable. This is known as "*Chevron* deference."
- Though the federal courts often base their judicial reviews of agency statutory interpretations on *Chevron* deference, not all federal courts—including the Supreme Court—have applied that approach on a consistent basis.
- In the federal courts, to obtain standing to sue, plaintiffs in environmental cases must demonstrate that they have suffered a concrete, particularized injury in fact that was "fairly traceable" to the defendant's actions. They must also show that a favorable decision is likely to "redress" their harm, and that their grievance arguably falls within the zone of interests protected or regulated by the statute or constitutional guarantee at issue in the lawsuit.
- In many state courts, to obtain standing to sue in environmental cases, plaintiffs must also demonstrate that they have been harmed to a greater extent than the rest of the general public, and/or that their injury was pecuniary in nature.
- In federal environmental cases, harm to aesthetic and environmental interests is a sufficient basis for demonstrating a concrete particularized injury in fact, whether or not the plaintiff has also suffered economic or financial injury.
- NGO plaintiffs in environmental litigation must show that at least some of the organization's members make use of the natural resource that is allegedly threatened by the defendant's present or planned conduct.
- Affidavits of members of an NGO averring that the affiants intend to return to an allegedly threatened resource at an unspecified future time are insufficient to demonstrate that a plaintiff NGO has suffered an injury in fact.

- In contrast, affidavits by members of a plaintiff NGO averring that their recreational, aesthetic, and/or economic interest will be harmed by a defendant's pollution do provide sufficient documentation of an injury in fact.
- Alleged interference with a plaintiff's commercial interest can be a sufficient basis for showing an injury in fact in a lawsuit based on the Endangered Species Act, at least in cases where the plaintiff has alleged that a federal agency failed to use the best scientific and commercial data available in implementing that Act.
- States are entitled to "special solicitude" in demonstrating their standing to sue in environmental litigation, particularly where they have alleged a risk of harm to their sovereign territory.
- Plaintiffs in environmental lawsuits must achieve at least some success on the merits to be eligible for an award of attorneys' fees.
- The amount of a prevailing plaintiff's fees in environmental cases must be based upon a "lodestar figure," i.e., reasonable hours worked by the attorney multiplied by a reasonable hourly billing rate. The lodestar figure may not be enhanced where a plaintiff has arranged to pay the plaintiff's attorney on a contingency fee basis.
- In environmental suits, injunctions are generally limited to circumstances where the plaintiff has suffered an irreparable injury for which there is no legal remedy, the defendant will not be harmed more than the plaintiff by the issuance of an injunction, and an injunction will serve the public interest.
- Injunctive relief is an equitable remedy that is not awarded lightly, and courts generally have considerable discretion in deciding whether an injunction will do justice between the parties and, if so, what the terms of an injunction are to be.
- However, in circumstances where Congress has made its legislative priorities clear, courts have no choice but to grant an injunction that conforms to Congress' intent.

Mastering Environmental Law Master Checklist

Clean Air Act (Chapter 2)

- ❑ The common law doctrines of nuisance and trespass have retained vitality as sources of law regarding air pollution problems.
- ❑ Courts vary in the approaches they have taken with respect to the remedy to be awarded successful plaintiffs in common law air pollution nuisance cases.
- ❑ "Criteria pollutants" are air pollutants from different sources that may reasonably be expected to endanger public health or welfare.
- ❑ The Clean Air Act requires EPA to identify criteria pollutants and to prepare "air quality criteria" documents for each identified criteria pollutant that indicate the effects on public health and welfare of those pollutants and techniques available to control their emission.
- ❑ EPA must also establish National Ambient Air Quality Standards for each criteria pollutant reflecting the level of air purity necessary to protect the public health (with an adequate margin of safety) and the public welfare. Areas that have air cleaner than the standards required are deemed "attainment areas." Dirtier air regions are known as "nonattainment areas."
- ❑ Considerations of economic costs may play no part in the setting of health-based National Ambient Air Quality Standards.
- ❑ Individual states are required to adopt State Implementation Plans containing enforceable emissions limitations that will result in the implementation and maintenance of National Ambient Air Quality Standards.

- ❑ State Implementation Plans must be submitted to EPA for review. Where the federal agency determines that a state's plan is inconsistent with the Act, EPA may create a binding Federal Implementation Plan for the control of criteria pollutants in the state.
- ❑ The Clean Air Act is technology-forcing legislation, i.e., legislation designed to force regulated entities to develop and use new pollution control devices and techniques where such techniques are not technically or economically feasible.
- ❑ The current Clean Air Act contains an extensive list of hazardous air pollutants.
- ❑ EPA is required to publish a listing of all categories and subcategories of major sources of all listed hazardous air pollutants and to develop maximum available control technology standards for those sources.
- ❑ New and modified sources of air pollutants in nonattainment areas must meet New Source Performance Standards (requiring the use of best demonstrated control technology in each source category) and New Source Review (mandating use of air pollution control technology that will achieve the "lowest achievable emission rate" and "offsets" to any new pollution those new or modified sources will create through reductions of pollutant emissions from existing sources).
- ❑ In attainment areas, new or modified sources must meet both New Source Performance Standards and Prevention of Significant Deterioration Standards.
- ❑ Under Prevention of Significant Deterioration requirements, states are required to classify their attainment areas based on how clean their air is.
- ❑ Entities that wish to construct new or modified sources in attainment areas must obtain preconstruction permits requiring, among other things, the use of the best available control technology.
- ❑ As directed by Congress, EPA has created new motor vehicle emissions standards that reflect the greatest degree of emission reduction achievable throughout the useful life of the vehicle.
- ❑ EPA is required to test samples of new cars, which must be supplied by auto manufacturers, for compliance with applicable standards.

- ❑ Passing EPA's tests is a prerequisite to obtain the "Certificate of Conformity" that is required before a vehicle may legally be sold in the United States.

Climate Change (Chapter 3)

- ❑ While the United States does not have a federal climate change statute, it uses a collection of other international, federal, and state environmental laws to require tracking, reporting, and control of greenhouse gas emissions.
- ❑ The United States has announced its desire to withdraw from the Paris Agreement, which is currently the leading international agreement for climate change actions by the international community.
  - ❑ The United States, however, remains a signatory to the U.N. Framework Convention on Climate Change, and it remains a member to the Paris Agreement under its terms until 2020.
  - ❑ The Paris Agreement does not impose any substantive emissions limits itself, and the United States can choose how it wishes to satisfy its general commitments under the Agreement.
- ❑ Although the U.S. Supreme Court has held that greenhouse gases are "pollutants" subject to regulation under the federal Clean Air Act, the Court struck down EPA's attempt to require permits for facilities that emit only greenhouse gases.
  - ❑ The Court has also stayed EPA's Clean Power Plan regulations, which would have limited emissions of greenhouse gases from fossil-fueled power plants under the Clean Air Act's performance standard program for new and existing sources.
  - ❑ It remains unclear the extent to which EPA can, or will, regulate greenhouse gases from facilities that also emit other regulated pollutants.
- ❑ As a result of electoral outcomes, the federal government has suspended or withdrawn several regulatory initiatives to regulate greenhouse gas emissions. These efforts include a proposal to formally overturn the Clean Power Plan regulations, a withdrawal of guidances and memoranda on the social cost of carbon emissions, and ways to account for greenhouse gas emissions in environmental impact statements.

- ❑ Other federal environmental statutes, including the Endangered Species Act and the Clean Water Act, may have limited applicability in requiring actions to mitigate or prevent climate change. But long-term climate change effects can affect the scope of protection offered to species threatened by climate change or to protections required for waters of the United States affected by climate change.
- ❑ The National Environmental Policy Act requires an assessment of the environmental impacts of major actions by the federal government, and this assessment may include a review of potential impacts by or to climate change.
- ❑ Tort law actions against emitters of greenhouse gases may not proceed under federal common law because the federal Clean Air Act has displaced those types of lawsuits. It remains to be seen whether state or local governmental plaintiffs can successfully pursue similar claims under solely state law in state or federal courts.
- ❑ Similarly, public trust doctrine lawsuits to force more aggressive actions by the government against climate change are actively underway in federal court, but have not yet yielded a definitive verdict or award.

Clean Water Act (Chapter 4)

- ❑ The Clean Water Act prohibits any discharge of a pollutant to navigable waters through a point source.
  - ❑ Any owner or operator of a facility that wants to discharge wastewaters into a water body under federal jurisdiction must first obtain an NPDES permit from EPA or a state agency in delegated states.
  - ❑ Some of the Act's terms—"discharge," "pollutant," "point source," and "navigable waters"—have specific regulatory definitions that mirror the broad statutory definition for each term, but that incorporate important exceptions.
    - NPDES permits are not required for discharges that simply move water within a water body without adding pollutants, or that go to isolated water bodies that do not constitute "navigable waters."
    - NPDES permits also are not needed for discharges vented solely to groundwater unconnected with navigable waters.

- ❑ NPDES permits establish specific limits for pollutants in the discharge based on both technology standards set by EPA and on whether the receiving water is clean enough for its selected use, as reflected in state water quality standards and total maximum daily loads.
- ❑ NPDES permits typically last for five years, and they must be renewed if the discharge continues past that time.

❑ If a facility does not discharge its effluent directly into navigable waters and instead sends it off-site to a centralized wastewater treatment plant or publicly owned treatment works (POTW), it must first satisfy pretreatment standards.

- ❑ The POTW operator will give the facility operator a permit or contract that spells out the specific contaminants (and concentrations of them) that the facility's effluent can contain.
- ❑ In addition, the effluent cannot disrupt the POTW's operations by creating either a bypass (where the pollutants pass through untreated) or upset (where the pollutants impair or shut down the POTW's treatment process).
- ❑ The POTW operator discharges under its own NPDES permit for its treatment process. If a facility's effluent causes the POTW operator to violate its permit, the POTW may either bring an enforcement action or initiate a breach of contract lawsuit against the facility if its discharges violated the POTW's pretreatment agreement or order.

❑ In addition to setting discharge limits on a site-by-site basis, the state must also identify whether the receiving water body is already impaired by other discharges and pollution.

- ❑ If that water body is impaired because its current pollution levels make it unfit for its designated use, the state must determine how much pollution that water body can safely absorb on a daily basis. The state then uses this number to set the Total Maximum Daily Load (TMDL) limit for the water body.
- ❑ EPA or the state will then back-calculate how much additional pollution a discharging facility will need to remove from an effluent stream to bring the water body into compliance with the applicable water quality standard. This can require additional reductions beyond the existing NPDES permit's treatment requirements.

- ❑ The Clean Water Act also restricts the placement of dredge and fill materials into wetlands under federal jurisdiction, unless pursuant to a permit.
    - ❑ These permits, authorized under Section 404 of the Clean Water Act, are issued by the U.S. Army Corps of Engineers. But EPA retains authority to veto proposed Section 404 permits that do not meet environmental standards.
    - ❑ Determining whether a wetland falls within "navigable waters" regulated under the Clean Water Act is often a difficult task, and it has generated heated and lengthy controversy in rulemaking proceedings as well as frequent litigation.
- ❑ Owners or operators of facilities or vessels must report a spill or release of a pollutant or oil to navigable waters under the Clean Water Act. Spills become reportable if they exceed a reportable quantity within a 24-hour period (although an operator must report a spill immediately once it exceeds the regulatory threshold). EPA has set reportable quantities for more than 300 chemicals by regulation; and a spill of oil to waters must be reported if it creates a sheen or slick on the water.
- ❑ In addition to enforcement actions by the state agency, operators who violate their NPDES permits may face administrative actions or lawsuits from EPA or citizen suits. The Clean Water Act authorizes citizens to sue permit holders for violating their permit's terms. Citizens may also sue EPA for failure to perform a nondiscretionary duty under the statute.

Comprehensive Environmental Response Compensation and Liability Act (CERCLA) (Chapter 5)

- ❑ EPA's response action process has multiple steps, including:
    - ❑ Preliminary assessment/site investigation at a reportedly contaminated hazardous substance facility.
    - ❑ A short-term "removal action" (if necessary).
    - ❑ Assessment of risk through a standard "hazard ranking system."
    - ❑ Listing on the National Priorities List for remedial action (where appropriate).
    - ❑ Preparation of a remedial investigation/feasibility study.

    - ❑ Selection of a clean-up remedy that is memorialized in a Record of Decision.
    - ❑ Design and implementation of a remedial design/remedial action.
    - ❑ Delisting of the facility from the National Priorities List.
    - ❑ Continued operation and maintenance activities at the facility (where needed).
- ❑ CERCLA creates potential liability for four categories of parties:
    - ❑ Present owners or operators of hazardous substance facilities.
    - ❑ Past owners or operators of facilities at which hazardous substances were disposed during their period of ownership or operation.
    - ❑ Parties that arranged for disposal or treatment of their hazardous substances by another.
    - ❑ Persons who accepted hazardous substances for transport to facilities or incineration sites from which there is a hazardous substance release.
- ❑ PRPs may be liable for:
    - ❑ Response costs incurred by government entities.
    - ❑ Response costs of nongovernment parties.
    - ❑ Natural resource damages.
    - ❑ Health assessment costs.
- ❑ In most cases, PRPs are strictly, joint and severally, and retroactively liable for cleanup costs, particularly (though not exclusively) where different hazardous substances have comingled at contaminated facilities.
- ❑ In a small minority of cases, PRPs have succeeded in avoiding joint and several liability by proving the divisibility of harm at hazardous substance facilities.
- ❑ CERCLA provides a cause of action for contribution for jointly and severally liable PRPs who seek to recover a fairer share of a common liability from other PRPs.
- ❑ Courts allocate response costs in contribution suits based upon whatever equitable factors the courts deem appropriate.

- ❑ Parties may only sue other parties for contribution where they have themselves been subject to a government enforcement action, or entered into a settlement with a government entity.
- ❑ In circumstances where it has not been subject to government enforcement action, any nongovernmental party may recover any money it has expended to clean up a contaminated facility under a separate provision of CERCLA that does not create a statutory right to contribution.
- ❑ CERCLA imposes certain substantial and procedural limitations with respect to settlements in remedial actions:
  - ❑ Only qualified persons may be permitted to prepare remedial investigation/feasibility studies.
  - ❑ Settlements calling for PRP performance of remedial actions may not contain general releases of liability.
  - ❑ PRPs may be granted covenants not to sue, subject to "re-opener provisions."
  - ❑ Remedial settlements must include stipulated penalties where agreed-upon obligations are not fulfilled by PRPs.
  - ❑ Settlement agreements must be in the form of a Consent Decree, to be approved by a federal judge following public notice and comment.
- ❑ Courts will typically approve consent decrees in CERCLA remedial cases where the settlement is fair, reasonable, and faithful to the goals of the statute.

Resource Conservation and Recovery Act (RCRA) (Chapter 6)

- ❑ Subtitle D of RCRA bans "open dumps" and requires that non-hazardous solid waste be deposited in "sanitary landfills," consistent with EPA-established criteria.
- ❑ The collection and disposal of solid waste is meant to take place at the state and local level, with guidance and assistance from EPA.
- ❑ Subtitle C of RCRA is intended to protect human health and the environment from the risks created by hazardous waste.
- ❑ The statutory definition of "hazardous waste" requires that, to be considered hazardous, a waste must first satisfy the statute's definition of a

"solid waste." EPA interprets "solid waste" broadly to include materials that are semi-solid, liquid, contained gases, or improperly recycled.

- ❑ EPA's subtitle C regulations identify two types of hazardous waste: characteristic hazardous waste (which has one or more hazardous characteristics) and listed hazardous waste (which EPA has specifically identified as hazardous).
- ❑ EPA established regulations for hazardous waste characteristics that can be detected by the use of a standard test method: ignitability, reactivity, corrosiveness, and toxicity.
- ❑ Seventeen specific wastes types (including household wastes and many mining wastes) have been excluded by Congress and/or EPA from RCRA Subtitle C regulation.
- ❑ EPA's RCRA regulations contain specific requirements that apply to generators and transporters of hazardous waste and to owners and operators of treatment, storage, and disposal facilities (TSDFs).
- ❑ The statute and EPA's regulations discourage the land disposal of hazardous waste, require "corrective action" where hazardous chemicals escape from TSDFs, and impose technical and financial assurance requirements on regulated facilities.
- ❑ Under RCRA, persons who own, operate, or plan to construct a new TSDF must obtain a permit to do so.
- ❑ Facilities in existence prior to the enactment of RCRA were allowed to continue to operate temporarily, in an "interim status," so long as they complied with interim status standards and filed a permit application.
- ❑ EPA's regulations impose numerous, strict requirements on owners and operators of TSDFs with regard to such matters as hazardous waste sampling and monitoring, recordkeeping, employee training, preventing and responding to emergency events, and closure and post-closure procedures.
- ❑ Individual states may be authorized to administer hazardous waste programs that are "equivalent" to the federal program, consistent with other states' programs, and have adequate provisions for enforcement.
- ❑ RCRA contemplates enforcement action by three types of actors: the federal government, states, and private citizens.

- ❑ EPA is authorized to take three distinct types of enforcement actions: administrative and (through the Department of Justice) civil judicial, and criminal.
- ❑ States that have been authorized to implement an RCRA hazardous waste management program must have enacted state laws that provide enforcement tools equivalent to those available to EPA.
- ❑ Private citizens may (after giving prior written notice) commence civil judicial actions against violators of RCRA requirements. However, such suits are barred where EPA or a state is "diligently prosecuting" a civil or criminal action to require compliance.

Regulation of Toxic Substances and Pesticides (Chapter 7)

- ❑ Distribution of chemicals subject to TSCA:
  - ❑ Manufacturing, but typically only for a commercial purpose.
  - ❑ Processing, which can include any person who prepares a chemical substance or mixture *after* its manufacture, but again only for distribution in commerce (i.e., for a commercial purpose).
  - ❑ "Using" the chemical in a manufacturing process, which TSCA does not define, and EPA has not promulgated a regulatory definition to narrow the term.
  - ❑ Importation of chemicals, which is classified as manufacturing.
- ❑ TSCA requires EPA to maintain a master inventory of all chemicals used in commerce. To add or modify a chemical's inventory listing, TSCA requires manufacturers or importers to obtain either a Premanufacturing Notice (for new chemicals) or a Significant New Use Registration (for existing chemicals). At either of these registration steps EPA can require an applicant to provide data or testing to EPA upon the Agency's request.
- ❑ EPA can require manufacturers and importers to test their chemicals and submit data under testing orders. In addition, they may also have an obligation under TSCA to report data or information about significant risks or adverse effects.
- ❑ FIFRA requires manufacturers to register their pesticides with EPA and obtain labels that prescribe the correct ways to use them.
  - ❑ Applicants must submit comprehensive test and safety data on the exact formulation of the pesticide and exactly how it will be

used. Future labels will approve only the uses set out in the data, and other uses or formulations are not approved.

- ❑ Parties may only use pesticides according to the instructions and warnings on their EPA-approved labels. Failure to do so violates FIFRA and can trigger both civil and criminal liability.
- ❑ Only certified applicators can buy and use substances that EPA has classified as "restricted pesticides."
- ❑ EPA is authorized to cancel or suspend a registration if the substance poses either an unwarranted risk (for cancellations) or an imminent hazard (for suspensions) to human health or the environment.
- ❑ EPA regulatory requirements and approved labeling can preempt conflicting state law requirements, but states may still impose some place and use restrictions on where and how pesticides are used. EPA-approved labels may preempt some state law tort claims as well, but that preemption by label does not extend to other facets of the pesticide, such as product defects or substandard testing.

National Environmental Policy Act (NEPA) (Chapter 8)

- ❑ NEPA contains broad, strongly pro-environmental statements of purposes and policies.
- ❑ NEPA includes an "interpretation mandate" that directs that "policies, regulations and public laws of the United States" be interpreted in accordance with the Act's broad policies. This sub-section has vast potential as a mechanism for eliciting environmentally sensitive interpretations of a range of federal laws.
- ❑ The statute has several "action-forcing" provisions, the most significant of which is its requirement that federal agencies and departments prepare a detailed environmental impact statement ("EIS") for every proposal for a "major federal action" significantly affecting the quality of the human environment.
- ❑ Courts have generally held that the procedural provisions of NEPA established a "strict standard of compliance" for federal agencies. This judicial rule is intended to compel agencies to advise and inform other interested agencies, and the public, of the environmental consequences of planned federal actions, and also to aid the agency's own decisionmaking.

- ❑ EISs must be considered at every important stage of an agency's decision making process.
- ❑ Citizen plaintiffs may bring suit through the Administrative Procedure Act to challenge an agency's failure to follow NEPA's procedural mandates and/or the adequacy of a final EIS.
- ❑ The U.S. Supreme Court has ruled that while reviewing courts may review agencies' compliance with EIS procedures, the substantive decisions reached by agencies following procedurally appropriate preparation of EISs—including decisions regarding possible mitigation measures—are not subject to judicial review under NEPA.
- ❑ NEPA created a Council on Environmental Quality ("CEQ") in the Executive Branch that has published regulations that guide federal agencies in the implementation of the Act.
- ❑ CEQ's regulations, and judicial interpretations, have fleshed out the meaning of the statutory phrases "major federal action" and "significantly affecting the quality of the human environment."
- ❑ "Major federal actions" generally involve federal actions that deal with the adoption of official policies, form a plan or program, or approve specific public or private projects.
- ❑ CEQ's regulations require agencies to divide their proposals for major federal actions into those that normally require an EIS, those that normally do not require an EIS, and those that may or may not require an EIS.
- ❑ Agency actions that normally do not require preparation of an EIS because they will predictably have no significant environmental impact are classified as "categorical exclusions."
- ❑ In circumstances where an agency action may or may not require preparation of an EIS, the agency must prepare a brief "Environmental Assessment" to determine whether or not to prepare an EIS.
- ❑ Environmental Assessments must lead to either the preparation of a full EIS or a "Finding of No Significant Impact."
- ❑ CEQ's regulations define the statutory term "significantly" in terms of both the context and intensity (i.e., severity of impact) of a proposed action.

- ❑ In preparing EISs, agencies must follow procedures set forth in detail in CEQ's regulations, which include "scoping" what the EIS will contain, circulating a draft EIS for comments from stakeholders, and preparing, circulating, and filing a final EIS.
- ❑ Typical judicial remedies for procedural violations of an EIS tend to require agencies to take additional procedural measures.
- ❑ NEPA litigation frequently involves motions for preliminary injunctions under Federal Rule of Civil Procedure 65. The proponents of those motions must satisfy four conditions to succeed in persuading courts to issue preliminary injunctions, including a showing that they are likely to succeed on the merits of the case. Such injunctions are not granted lightly.

Endangered and Protected Species (Chapter 9)

- ❑ The Endangered Species Act protects only species that the federal government has affirmatively listed as either endangered or threatened.
- ❑ The U.S. Fish & Wildlife Service (F&WS) or the National Marine Fisheries Service (NMFS) will list a species as endangered or threatened based on the best available scientific and commercial data, but they will not base the listing decision on the economic value of the species. However, they may consider economic impacts in identifying the critical habitat that the species will require to survive.
- ❑ A federal agency may not take actions that will jeopardize an endangered or threatened species. To determine if its action will jeopardize the species, a federal agency must consult with either the F&WS or NMFS. Those agencies in turn will produce a biological opinion. If the biological opinion finds that the action will jeopardize a protected species (even with mitigation or protective actions), the federal agency is not permitted to move ahead with the action.
- ❑ If the agency's action is otherwise legal, and it only causes the incidental death of some protected species members without threatening the species overall, the agency may obtain authorization for an incidental take of the species, consistent with the biological opinion.
- ❑ Any person (including private parties and federal agencies) who knowingly causes the taking of a protected land animal or fish (and, in some cases, a plant) may face civil and criminal liability under

Section 9 of the Endangered Species Act. Among other things, this prohibition includes taking a species through the destruction or impairment of critical habitat needed by the species.

- ❑ If a person will only incidentally take some protected species members as part of an otherwise legal action, he or she may seek an Incidental Take Permit that would authorize the taking. Such permits require the submission of a Habitat Conservation Plan that would assure the protection of the protected species.
- ❑ The Marine Mammal Protection Act also prohibits the taking of members of marine species (including whales, dolphins, walruses, seals, sea lions, and polar bears) in marine waters under U.S. jurisdiction. Some exceptions to this prohibition allow limited incidental takes of some species, including hunts for subsistence needs by native American tribes and scientific research.
- ❑ The Migratory Bird Treaty Act protects migratory birds, including a vast array of songbirds, waterfowl, and common birds. This Act relies solely on criminal liability for enforcement, and its reduced requirements for misdemeanor criminal liability makes it an important environmental enforcement tool after spills or releases that injure migratory birds.

Environmental Enforcement (Chapter 10)

- ❑ Self-monitoring and self-reporting of their concentrations of effluents and discharges and related matters by regulated pollution sources are common and important features of environmental regulation.
- ❑ Regulated parties that have self-reported violations of an environmental standard may not excuse their reported noncompliance by showing sampling or laboratory errors.
- ❑ Where owners or operators of regulated sources of pollution object to the entry of a government inspector onto their facility, the government must usually obtain a search warrant. Such a warrant may be based upon a showing that the business in question was selected for inspection based upon a general administrative plan for enforcement derived from neutral sources.
- ❑ Administrative enforcement represents a large proportion of the enforcement activities of many agencies.

- ❑ Notices of Violation are warning documents that simply bring an environmental violation to the attention of the violator and request compliance.
- ❑ Administrative Compliance Orders are enforceable orders that require regulated parties to achieve compliance with environmental requirements consistent with a detailed timetable.
- ❑ Administrative Penalty Orders are used to directly assess specific monetary penalties against environmental violators. The rights of parties who receive such orders vary by jurisdiction, agency, and statute.
- ❑ The precise elements that the government must prove by a preponderance of evidence in a civil enforcement case vary from statute to statute.
- ❑ Typically, environmental statutes establish a regime of strict liability and the government need not prove environmental harm to make out a *prima facie* case.
- ❑ In civil enforcement actions, affirmative defenses are usually limited and difficult to establish.
- ❑ Where the government seeks civil penalties for environmental violations, a five-year statute of limitations generally applies, although there are some specific exceptions.
- ❑ Since the 1980s, most federal environmental statutes have included felony crimes that carry the potential for fines and imprisonment for more than 12 months.
- ❑ Prosecutors sometimes also charge general federal crimes in cases that involve alleged environmental crimes.
- ❑ Several federal environmental statutes have been deemed public welfare statutes. *Mens rea* need not be proven by government when it criminally enforces those statutes.
- ❑ Where environmental statutes require proof that a defendant "knowingly" violated the law, courts have held that the statutory term "knowingly" simply connotes awareness on a defendant's part that the defendant engaged in the prohibited acts that formed the basis for the criminal prosecution.

- ❑ Numerous affirmative defenses may be raised in environmental criminal enforcement cases, from challenges to the statute's constitutionality to entrapment, double jeopardy, statutorily created defenses, and others.

- ❑ The Fifth Amendment double jeopardy clause has been held to bar only additional prosecutions by the same sovereign. The clause does not bar separate federal and state prosecutions for the same environmental offense.

- ❑ Plaintiffs in citizen enforcement suits must satisfy a number of procedural requirements, including a demonstration of standing to sue, a pre-filing notice, statutory jurisdiction, the absence of mootness, and statutory preclusion.

- ❑ Nearly all environmental statutory citizen suit provisions require that citizen plaintiffs provide both the alleged violator and government officials with a written notice of intent to sue at least 60 days before filing suit. This notice requirement has been deemed a mandatory precondition to suit.

- ❑ Where a federal statute authorizes citizen suits against a party "alleged to be in violation" of an environmental requirement, citizen plaintiffs must allege either continuous or intermittent violations. Under those circumstances, citizen suits for wholly past violations are not permitted.

- ❑ The U.S. Supreme Court has held that defendants in environmental citizen enforcement cases raising a defense of mootness have a "formidable burden" of showing that it is "absolutely clear" that their alleged noncompliance will not recur.

- ❑ Nearly all environmental statutory citizen suit provisions bar citizen suits where the defendant can demonstrate that a government agency is "diligently prosecuting" the defendant for the same violation.

Environmental Litigation and Pertinent Administrative Law (Chapter 11)

- ❑ In lawsuits to slow or halt projects that are alleged to harm the environment, courts will sometimes apply "hard look review." This judicial approach requires agencies to justify their actions by preparing a complete administrative record that demonstrates that the agency has carefully considered all relevant factors and avoided clear errors of judgment.

- ❑ In conducting hard look review, courts may not substitute their own views for those of the defendant agency. However, reviewing courts must make a "searching and careful" review of the factual basis for the agency's decision, and they must remand the matter to the agency if they determine that it has made clear errors of judgment.
- ❑ The federal courts generally take a relatively deferential posture when they review agency interpretations of a statute that the agency is charged with administering. When Congress has spoken directly to the precise question at issue, a reviewing court (and the agency) must give effect to Congress's intent.
- ❑ Where Congress has not spoken directly to the question at issue, however, a reviewing court must defer to the statutory interpretation of the implementing agency as long as that interpretation is permissible and reasonable. This is known as "*Chevron* deference."
- ❑ Though the federal courts often base their judicial reviews of agency statutory interpretations on *Chevron* deference, not all federal courts—including the Supreme Court—have applied that approach on a consistent basis.
- ❑ In the federal courts, to obtain standing to sue, plaintiffs in environmental cases must demonstrate that they have suffered a concrete, particularized injury in fact that was "fairly traceable" to the defendant's actions. They must also show that a favorable decision is likely to "redress" their harm, and that their grievance arguably falls within the zone of interests protected or regulated by the statute or constitutional guarantee at issue in the lawsuit.
- ❑ In many state courts, to obtain standing to sue in environmental cases, plaintiffs must also demonstrate that they have been harmed to a greater extent than the rest of the general public, and/or that their injury was pecuniary in nature.
- ❑ In federal environmental cases, harm to aesthetic and environmental interests is a sufficient basis for demonstrating a concrete particularized injury in fact, whether or not the plaintiff has also suffered economic or financial injury.
- ❑ NGO plaintiffs in environmental litigation must show that at least some of the organization's members make use of the natural resource that is allegedly threatened by the defendant's present or planned conduct.

- ❑ Affidavits of members of an NGO averring that the affiants intend to return to an allegedly threatened resource at an unspecified future time are insufficient to demonstrate that a plaintiff NGO has suffered an injury in fact.
- ❑ In contrast, affidavits by members of a plaintiff NGO averring that their recreational, aesthetic, and/or economic interest will be harmed by a defendant's pollution do provide sufficient documentation of an injury in fact.
- ❑ Alleged interference with a plaintiff's commercial interest can be a sufficient basis for showing an injury in fact in a lawsuit based on the Endangered Species Act, at least in cases where the plaintiff has alleged that a federal agency failed to use the best scientific and commercial data available in implementing that Act.
- ❑ States are entitled to "special solicitude" in demonstrating their standing to sue in environmental litigation, particularly where they have alleged a risk of harm to their sovereign territory.
- ❑ Plaintiffs in environmental lawsuits must achieve at least some success on the merits to be eligible for an award of attorneys' fees.
- ❑ The amount of a prevailing plaintiff's fees in environmental cases must be based upon a "lodestar figure," i.e., reasonable hours worked by the attorney multiplied by a reasonable hourly billing rate. The lodestar figure may not be enhanced where a plaintiff has arranged to pay the plaintiff's attorney on a contingency fee basis.
- ❑ In environmental suits, injunctions are generally limited to circumstances where the plaintiff has suffered an irreparable injury for which there is no legal remedy, the defendant will not be harmed more than the plaintiff by the issuance of an injunction, and an injunction will serve the public interest.
- ❑ Injunctive relief is an equitable remedy that is not awarded lightly, and courts generally have considerable discretion in deciding whether an injunction will do justice between the parties and, if so, what the terms of an injunction are to be.
- ❑ However, in circumstances where Congress has made its legislative priorities clear, courts have no choice but to grant an injunction that conforms to Congress' intent.

Index